Nancy Wier

BRIDGE: MODERN BIDDING

BRIDGE:
MODERN BIDDING

by
VICTOR MOLLO

FABER AND FABER
24 Russell Square
London

First published in mcmlxi
by Faber and Faber Limited
24 Russell Square London W.C.1
New, revised edition mcmlxvi
Printed in Great Britain by
Latimer, Trend & Co. Ltd Whitstable

CONTENTS

CONTENTS

CONTENTS

AUTHOR'S PREFACE TO THE SECOND EDITION

By the nature of things, a text book is an exposition of theory. In this edition of Modern Bidding, I have tried to break new ground by bringing before the reader the finished product, the practice on which all theory is based.

The first part of the book describes, as before, the modern bidding alphabet. The new section, which follows, shows how the letters of that alphabet are put together into the words of the bidding language by the world's best players. All my illustrations are taken from the 1965 World Championship at Buenos Aires, made famous by the accusations of cheating brought by the Americans against Britain's leading pair, Terence Reese and Boris Schapiro. All the hands I reproduce were bid by this pair and all were used at the London enquiry to support or to refute the accusations.

In selecting my examples I had a twofold purpose: to let the reader see and judge for himself the hands that gave rise to the greatest bridge scandal of our day; and to give him a close-up view of tactics—of that unceasing battle of wits, which is so often more important than technical considerations in deciding the result of matches in top class bridge.

Most of the conventions in popular use today, and especially the latest and most promising innovations, are outlined in the first fifteen chapters of this book. By and large, my main concern has been not with artificial gadgets, but with the basic structure of bidding, which does not and cannot change.

Too many books have been written about too many systems and too few about the broad framework of bidding to which all systems must conform—or perish.

I was brought up myself the Acol way, in the philosophy

which has shaped British bidding over the past thirty years. I believe that for everyday purposes it is the best. At all levels, except in the rarified and exotic atmosphere of world championships, it has proved to be by far the most successful. And I feel certain that the keen bridge player will find it the easiest to absorb and, above all, the most enjoyable to put into practice.

1

MINIMUM OPENINGS AND
RESPONSES

Bidding is a language. Because its vocabulary consists of less than forty bids, each one must do a lot of work. How good are you? That, of course, is what partner wants to know most and you must try from the first to give him the measure of your strength.

Strength has two ingredients: High cards and Distribution. Both can be measured and co-related, and a picture of the whole can then be shown to partner.

The Point Count

To assess the value of high cards, there exists a world currency, the Milton Work Count, which lays down this scale:

An Ace counts 4　　　　A Queen counts 2
A King counts 3　　　　A Knave counts 1

Just as Aces and Kings take tricks, so do the small cards—sometimes as trumps, sometimes when a long suit has been established. For distributional values add 1 point for every card in excess of four in each suit. Thus: A 6 5 4 3 2 is worth 6 points—4 for the Ace and 2 more for the long cards.

A Minimum Opening

Without a 5-card suit a minimum opening is made on 13 (High Card) points. With a 5-card suit 12 is enough, for the total, after allowing a point for the long card, still comes to 13. Experts often open on less, but by and large, 13 High Card and Distributional points combined is the right strength for a minimum opening.

Part Score, Game or Slam?

The Point Count is a good guide, too, in telling the partnership whether it should stop in a part score or go on to game or to a slam. For a game, the two hands should add up to 25–26 and for a slam to 33–34.

With less than 25, stop in a part score contract, and if you are not going on to game, try to stop below the Three level, for it is easier to make eight tricks than nine.

Every Opening Promises a Rebid

An opening bid guarantees a rebid. Since the bidding vocabulary is strictly limited, it is rarely possible to describe a hand in one bid. To get together with partner may require two or more and the opener must, therefore, always bear in mind his *rebid*. This brings us to a cardinal principle of modern bidding: Unless partner has already passed, a response by him in a suit, different from the opener's, is *forcing* for one round. The opener *must* bid again.

Principle of Preparedness

It follows that it is not enough to count up to 13. Before making the first move the opener must think of the next one. His opening must be **prepared** for the rebid.

To make things easier for yourself, when you open the bidding, bear these precepts in mind:

1. A 5-card (or longer) suit is always prepared, because the same suit can be bid again, next time.
2. With two touching suits of equal length, e.g., Spades and Hearts, bid the *higher*-ranking suit first, regardless of quality. Again, your opening will be prepared, for on the next round you can bid your second suit without raising the level.
3. Any 4-card suit headed by the Q 10 is *biddable*, and at a pinch, you can shade that too.

4. An opening of 1 Club is *always* prepared. Partner is able to respond in any suit at the One level and opener can then call 1 No Trump, keeping the bidding low.

Hence the expression, **Prepared Club**, which means that if you think your rebid will present a problem, you may open on a 3-card Club suit.

Rebids after Minimum Openings

(1)	(2)	(3)
♠ 9 8 6 5 2	♠ 6 5 4 3 2	♠ 6 5 4 3 2
♡ A K	♡ A K Q J	♡ A 4
◊ A 4 2	◊ K 3	◊ A K Q J
♣ K 5 3	♣ 3 2	♣ 3 2

On (1) you open 1 S and rebid 2 S on the next round over 2 H, 2 D or 2 C. You pass 1 No Trump. *Don't like to rebid such a weak Suit*

On (2) you open 1 S and rebid 2 H.

On (3) you open 1 S and rebid 2 S over 2 H, but 2 D over 2 C.

Note that each time you open your *longest* suit and not your best suit in terms of high cards.

Observe also that on (3), if partner responds 2 H, you have to suppress your diamonds altogether, because your hand is not strong enough to warrant a bid at the Three level.

(4)

♠ 7 5 4 2
♡ K Q 6 *5*
◊ Q J 10 *3*
♣ A Q 7 *6*

15–17

If you are playing a strong No Trump, ~~16–18~~ points, you open this hand 1 C. On the next round you will have the choice of raising partner's suit or of rebidding 1 No Trump. But you are not good enough to open 1 (strong) No Trump, and you have too much to pass.

Opening Sequence on Minimum Values—1

EXAMPLES

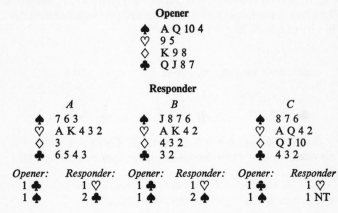

Opener

♠ A Q 10 4
♡ 9 5
◇ K 9 8
♣ Q J 8 7

Responder

A	B	C
♠ 7 6 3	♠ J 8 7 6	♠ 8 7 6
♡ A K 4 3 2	♡ A K 4 2	♡ A Q 4 2
◇ 3	◇ 4 3 2	◇ Q J 10
♣ 6 5 4 3	♣ 3 2	♣ 4 3 2

Opener:	Responder:	Opener:	Responder:	Opener:	Responder
1 ♣	1 ♡	1 ♣	1 ♡	1 ♣	1 ♡
1 ♠	2 ♣	1 ♠	2 ♠	1 ♠	1 NT

TABLE I

Opener	Count	Responder	Opener's Rebid
Without a 5-card suit open the bidding on **13** or a *good* **12**	0—5 5—8	No Bid. 1. a suit at the One level or 2. 1 NT (only if (1) is impracticable) or 3. —with four cards in partner's suit or three headed by the Ace, King or Queen—a SINGLE RAISE.	1. Another suit at One level or the level of Two, if it is lower ranking than the first suit. 2. 1 NT. 3. With a fit (see (3) in previous column) a single raise for Responder's suit. 4. Pass Responder's 1 NT.

14

Responses

On a weak hand, without support for Opener's suit or a 5-card suit of his own, Responder looks for a secondary fit. To allow the greatest room for manœuvre he makes the *cheapest* bid he can find. Responding to 1 C:

(1)	(2)	(3)
♠ A Q 10 3	♠ A K 7 2	♠ 10 9 8 4 2
♡ 8 4 2	♡ K 9 7 2	♡ A K Q J
◇ Q 10 3 2	◇ 8 4	◇ 8 4
♣ 7 2	♣ 5 4 2	♣ 6 3

On (1) the best bid is 1 D, not 1 S. This gives partner two chances. He can raise diamonds or he may be able to call 1 S himself. Over 1 S from Responder he may not be strong enough, even if he has the suit, to call Diamonds at the Two level, in which case a Diamond fit may be missed.

On (2) Responder should bid 1 H. This again gives partner two chances, to raise Hearts or to bid Spades—if he has four of them—at the One level.

Each time, the cheapest bid by Responder helps Opener in his rebid and improves the chances of finding a fit.

Showing Two Suits

Example (3) introduces a different element. This time Responder intends to show both majors, which he can do without going beyond the Two level. The sequence will be:

Opener	Responder
1 C	1 S
2 C (or 1 NT)	2 H

Note the inference:

With four cards in each major the response would have been 1 H, as in (2). Since Spades were bid first, then Hearts, Opener will be able to infer that Responder has *five* Spades.

Suit Response preferred to 1 NT

Opener calls 1 H. Responder holds:

	(4)		(5)
♠	Q J 9 8	♠	8 4 2
♡	7	♡	7 6
◊	K 9 8 7 3	◊	A Q 8 4 2
♣	10 8 3	♣	Q 3 2

On (4) he bids 1 S, not 2 D. He is not strong enough to bid at the Two level. Moreover it is more constructive to show a major than a minor.

On (5) the bid is 1 No Trump. Again Responder is reluctant to go beyond the One level, yet he is too strong to pass.

A response at the Two level—other than a raise of partner's suit—promises about 9 points, and a response at the level of Two in Hearts suggests nearly always a *5-card suit*. But a response at the level of One, as 1 S on (4), may be even weaker than 1 No Trump, once treated as a conventional denial bid. When practicable, respond with a One bid in a suit. It is more constructive than 1 NT.

Major before a Minor

	(6)
♠	J 7 6
♡	K 10 4 2
◊	Q 3
♣	J 6 3 2

On

respond 1 H to 1 D or 1 C. If you call 1 NT or 2 C (over 1 C) a fit in Hearts may be lost.

The general rule is:

⚹ With four cards in partner's major, raise it at once. With four (or five) cards in his minor try, first, to find a fit in a major.

16

MINIMUM OPENINGS AND RESPONSES

Opening Sequence on Minimum Values—2

EXAMPLES

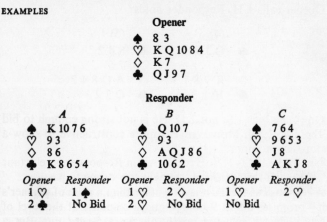

Opener

♠ 8 3
♡ K Q 10 8 4
◇ K 7
♣ Q J 9 7

Responder

A	B	C
♠ K 10 7 6	♠ Q 10 7	♠ 7 6 4
♡ 9 3	♡ 9 3	♡ 9 6 5 3
◇ 8 6	◇ A Q J 8 6	◇ J 8
♣ K 8 6 5 4	♣ 10 6 2	♣ A K J 8

Opener	Responder	Opener	Responder	Opener	Responder
1 ♡	1 ♠	1 ♡	2 ◇	1 ♡	2 ♡
2 ♣	No Bid	2 ♡	No Bid	No Bid	

TABLE II

Opener	Responder	Opener's Rebid
With a 5-card suit open the bidding on **12** and with a 6-card suit or two 5-card suits on **11** or a *good* **10**	You may show a 5-card suit at the Two level with **9** or more (including points for length). With less respond as in Table I.	1. The same suit again at the Two level. 2. A second suit if it can be shown at the One level or at the Two level, if it is *lower ranking* than the first suit. 3. With a fit, a single raise for Responder.

So long as this does not raise the level of the bidding, Opener should try to show a second suit even though it be shorter than the first.

Preference

Responder's first bid is a slow approach shot, designed to

17

leave room for the exchange of information. On the next round there may be no room left at a safe level to explore further. Then, if Opener has called two suits, Responder must choose the one he likes best—or dislikes least. This is known as giving preference and must never be confused with a voluntary raise.

Opener calls 1 H and over Responder's 1 S he bids 2 C.

Responder holds:

(7)	(8)	(9)
♠ K J 7 6	♠ K J 7 6	♠ K Q J 7
♡ 7 6 2	♡ A 2	♡ 7 6 2
♢ 9 7 6 4	♢ 9 7 6 4	♢ J 7 6
♣ A 2	♣ 7 6 2	♣ 7 6 2

On (7) Responder calls 2 H. This promises no support for Hearts, but shows that he prefers them to Clubs, because he is *longer*—not stronger—in that suit.

On (8) he is longer in Clubs and gives preference by *passing*.

On (9) he goes back to 2 H. With equal length in both suits preference is shown for the first. Opener may have more hearts than Clubs, but not the other way round.

Observe that apart from the first round response, no change of suit by Opener or Responder is, in itself, forcing. There are sequences in which a change of suit may be forcing *by inference*. We shall come to that later, when we hold better cards than we have done so far. Meanwhile, on minimum or near minimum holdings the focus should be on keeping the bidding low and on not going beyond the Two level until a good fit has been found.

Before passing on to the next chapter, the following points require to be underlined.

Keeping the Bidding Low

While Opener bids first the higher ranking of two touching suits, Responder does the opposite. The reason for this paradox is that Opener promises a rebid and Responder does not. To exchange the maximum information at the lowest level, each in turn, observes the principle of preparedness—but it applies in opposite ways.

Responding to a Minimum

You may keep the bidding open, occasionally, on as little as 5 points. But you are not expected to do so, and most of the time, if that is all you have, you will do best to pass. With a minimum make the cheapest response—e.g. 1 D over 1 C or 1 H over 1 D. Do not respond 1 NT over a minor without 6 or 7 points, if you can help it.

Measuring a Hand.

Is there a misprint in **Table 1**? The minimum for an opening is given as 13. Yet Opener's hand in the example above the chart adds up to only 12.

The answer is that the hand is *worth* 13. Firstly, the shape is 4–4–3–2, not the flat 4–3–3–3. Secondly, the middle cards—the tens and nines—swell the total by about a point.

Throughout this book a distinction will be made between *good* and *bad* hands with the same count in top cards—even when the distributional pattern is the same.

When 12 Equals 14

Every bridge player should acquire the habit of treating a *bad* 14 as no better than a *good* 12. This means in practice that a hand with 12 high card points and, say, a ten, two nines and two eights, is just as good as a 14 with no x higher than a 7.

In short, as Orwell might have said, all minimum openings are equal, but some are more equal than others.

2

LIMIT BIDS

If Responder keeps the bidding open on as little as 5–6 points it is—in part, at least—because his partner may have as many as 20. And if Opener promises a rebid, even on a minimum, it is because Responder, in turn, may have a hand worth 13 or more. Neither the opening nor the response is *limited*, except within very wide margins.

In certain well defined situations, however, the opposite applies. Bids and Responses are then *strictly limited*. A distinctive feature of British methods, which derive from the Acol system, is the frequent use of limit bids.

Quantitative Bidding

All No Trump responses, such as 2 NT over One of a suit, are limited. So are direct raises in partner's suit. This is known as quantitative bidding, because the bigger the hand, the bigger the bid.

If I open 1 Spade on a *minimum* and partner responds 3 Spades or 2 NT, I can and should pass, for I can tell that our combined values barely reach up to 25, the least we need for game. I know it, because Responder's hand is limited. He cannot have more than 12 and may well have 11. With 13 he would have called 4 Spades, not 3, or 3 NT, not 2.

Shape for Jump Responses

Responder tends to make limit bids on holdings which fall into two categories. First, the squat, balanced type with no void or singleton and no biddable major. Then he responds in

No Trumps. In the second category are hands which promise a good fit for partner's major. Opener calls 1 Heart or 1 Spade. Responder likes it. To show how much, he makes a single, double or treble raise, announcing at once the full extent of his support.

Measuring a Fit

A good fit for partner's suit depends on distribution—trump holding and ruffing value. That, in turn, depends on shortages—voids, singletons and doubletons. The Point Count is adapted to take in distributional values. Instead of adding points for long cards, apply this scale:

> 3 points for a void
> 2 points for a singleton
> 1 point for a doubleton.

These rates, which are on the conservative side, presuppose four prospective trumps. With three trumps only reduce them by about a third. With five inflate by nearly as much.

LIMIT BIDS

Limit Responses

Opener

♠ 6 4
♡ K Q 10 4 3 2
◇ A Q 6
♣ 9 2

Responder

A		B		C	
♠ A K Q 2		♠ Q J 10 2		♠ Q J 10	
♡ 9 7 6 5		♡ J 7		♡ J 7	
◇ 4		◇ K J 7		◇ K J 4 2	
♣ Q 8 4 3		♣ K 6 5 4		♣ A Q 5 3	

Opener	*Responder*	*Opener*	*Responder*	*Opener*	*Responder*
1 ♡	4 ♡	1 ♡	1 ♠	1 ♡	3 NT
No Bid		2 ♡	2 NT	4 ♡	No Bid
		3 ♡	No Bid		

TABLE III

Opener	Count	Responder	Opener's Rebid
One of a Major e.g. 1 H	11 or 12	With a balanced hand (no void or singleton) call 2 NT. With four (or five) Hearts call 3 H	With a minimum, balanced (i) PASS. (ii) With a 6-card suit, sign off over 2 NT in 3 H (see B above). With more than a minimum raise to GAME.
	13 or 14	3 NT or 4 H according to pattern.	On a distributional hand convert 3 NT into 4 H. This shows no extra strength (see C).

Lacking a fit for Opener's major, Responder can always show any biddable suit. He does not have to call 2 NT or 3 NT just because he has a given number of points.

Responses to a Minor

As we saw in the last chapter, responding to a minor is not quite the same thing as responding to a major. That is because on all but very distributional hands there is generally a cheaper game contract than 5 C or 5 D and the partnership tries to find it. Also, in competitive situations, a minor is too easily outbid by a major.

The sequence 1 H—3 H (or 1 S—3 S) usually leads to a game contract in a major. But the sequence 1 C—3 C (or 1 D—3 D) ends generally in 3 NT. It is sometimes easier to make ten tricks in a suit than nine in No Trumps, but between eleven tricks and nine there is quite a gulf.

A jump raise in a minor (1 C—3 C) denies a biddable major. No response in a major denies a fit—even an outstanding fit—in a minor.

A jump response in No Trumps—2 NT over 1 C or 3 NT over 1 D—*suggests* that Responder has no biddable major, though it does not expressly deny one, for there are other considerations to be taken into account, notably tenaces. The fact that the opening lead runs up to declarer may be all important on certain holdings.

Opener calls 1 C and Responder holds:

(1)	(2)	(3)
♠ K 7 6 2	♠ K 7 4	♠ K 7 6 2
♡ A 4 2	♡ A 10 2	♡ K J 3
◇ Q J 6	◇ K 7 6 2	◇ K J 9
♣ J 6 2	♣ J 6 2	♣ Q 4 2

On (1) he makes the natural response of 1 S, intending to call 2 NT next time over, say, 2 C.

On (2) there can be little object in showing the anaemic 4-card minor and Responder best describes his hand by calling 2 NT at once.

On (3) the Spades and the shape are identical with (1) and it is not wrong to call 1 S. The better bid, however, is 3 NT, for Responder would like the lead to run up to his tenaces in the red suits and his hand is so balanced that even if Opener has four Spades it may be easier to make nine tricks in No Trumps than ten in the major.

Signing Off

In one important respect minors and majors are handled alike. A rebid of the same suit at the lowest level always denotes weakness. Over a limit bid this takes the form of a Sign-Off—a virtual command to partner to pass.

If I respond 2 NT to opener's 1 C (or 1 S), and he bids 3 C (or 3 S), I can have nothing more to say. I have made a limit bid and partner knows, therefore, what I have. Knowing it, he has decided that 3 C (or 3 S) should be the *final contract*. I must defer to him, for he knows more about my hand than I know about his.

Change of Suit over 2 No Trumps

Note, however, that only a rebid in the *same* suit is a Sign-Off. If Opener calls another suit over 2 NT, that is unconditionally forcing. In the sequence:

Opener	Responder
1 H	2 NT
3 D	

the last bid is forcing on Responder.

With

(1)	(2)	(3)
♠ K 10 3	♠ K 10 3	♠ A 4
♡ 10 2	♡ 10 6 2	♡ K 10 3
◇ A J 6	◇ A J 6	◇ A 9 2
♣ K 8 4 3 2	♣ K 8 4 3	♣ 9 7 6 3 2

he calls 3 NT on (1), but 3 H on (2). Opener will not expect him to have more than three Hearts since with four he would have supported Hearts at once.

24

Opener's sequence suggests that he has a 5-card major and is looking for an alternative to No Trumps. Responder has limited his hand in two ways. He cannot have more than 11–12 high card points, and he cannot have four Hearts. It is up to him now to show that he has three Hearts.

On (3) he jumps over 3 D to 4 H. His hand is limited in the same way as before, but he likes *both* Opener's suits—in short, he has a good fit and his hand has *improved*. Hence the jump.

Another facet of this type of situation appears in the sequence:

Opener	Responder
1 C	1 H
1 S	2 NT
3 H	

Responder holds:

(4)

♠ A 7
♡ Q J 10 3 2
◇ J 6 2
♣ K 10 6

or

(5)

♠ A 9 7
♡ Q J 10 3
◇ J 6 2
♣ K 10 6

On (4) he calls 4 H, for he does not need to find partner with four trumps. Three should be enough. On (5) he calls 3 S. And on both hands he must avoid No Trumps, for by bidding two suits and supporting a third, Opener has shown an acute shortage in the fourth, Diamonds, which is Responder's weak spot, too.

Direct Raises in a Major

It is a cardinal principle of modern British bidding that with 4-card support for partner's major the suit is raised *directly*, on the first round. This gives rise to valuable inferences. Some of them can be seen in operation on the hands discussed in the preceding pages. Here is another:

Opener	Responder
1 H	1 S
2 D	3 H

Opener knows that his partner is good enough for a jump raise, but that he has only three Hearts. With four he would have bid 3 H at once.

Therefore

(1)	(2)
♠ A 2	♠ 10 4 2
♡ K Q J 6 5	♡ A K 8 6
◇ K Q 7 4	◇ A K J 2
♣ 10 4	♣ 7 3

On (1) he calls 4 H, but on (2) he bids 3 S, hoping to find Responder with five Spades.

Three Card Support

When declarer has only seven trumps between his own hand and dummy the chances are about 2–1 against the six outstanding cards being split 3–3 (it is a 36 per cent chance). The more likely (48 per cent) 4–2 division often proves embarrassing in the play of the hand, for if declarer is forced early he may lose trump control.

To avoid this danger many experienced players are reluctant to raise partner's suit, until he has rebid it, on less than four prospective trumps. This is sound—most of the time. In certain situations, however, it is correct, and tactically advantageous, to raise on three trumps only and there should be no inhibitions in doing so. The following are typical examples:

Opener calls 1 S and Responder holds:

(1)	(2)	(3)
♠ 10 7 6	♠ Q 6 5	♠ A 9 2
♡ 4	♡ 7 3	♡ 4 2
◇ A 10 7 6 4 2	◇ A J 9 6 3	◇ Q 10 7 6
♣ 8 6 3	♣ 9 6 2	♣ 8 6 3 2

(1) The shape is wrong for 1 NT and the high card strength falls short of the recognized minimum for any response other than No Bid. The ruffing value represented by the singleton Heart, however, just turns the scales and allows the hand to be stretched into a simple raise to 2 S. This is reinforced by another consideration. Opponents may have a Heart contract, but will not find it so easy to come in over 2 S. In the same situation, it would not be correct to raise a minor.

(2) The hand is worth a bid, but only one, and in such cases it is more constructive to support partner's major than to call 1 NT—the only alternative.

(3) Here 1 NT is in order, but since 2 S will have a superior pre-emptive value, it is the better bid.

There are exceptions to every rule, but by and large, observe this principle:

If partner opens a minor, never—unless opponents butt in—raise him with three cards only in his suit and avoid, whenever possible, raising him with less than five.

If he opens a major, try not to raise him with less than four-card support. Look for an alternative. But do not expect to succeed all the time, and remember that it is better to owe partner a trump than to fail to show a fit.

Delayed Game Raise

To the rule that a 4-card fit in a major should be shown at once there is an important exception. It is illustrated in the sequence:

Opener	Responder
1 H	1 S
2 C	4 H

On the face of it, this is self-contradictory. Opener has not shown more than four Hearts and with less than four himself Responder should not raise him to game. Yet with four Hearts he should have supported the suit at once. What happened?

The answer is that this paradox is constructed deliberately to show a raise to $4\frac{1}{2}$ Hearts.

27

Shape and Strength

Try responding to 1 S on:

(1)	(2)	(3)
♠ K 10 8 4	♠ K 10 8 4 2	♠ K 10 8 4
♡ A 8	♡ A 8	♡ A K 2
◇ K J 4 3	◇ 3	◇ 3 2
♣ Q 6 2	♣ A J 5 4 2	♣ K 10 9 8

(1) is a routine raise to 4 S, showing 4-card trump support and 13–14 points.

But (2) is a much better hand though the high card points add up to only 12. To show how much better it is than (1) Responder applies the Delayed Game Raise—a carefully contrived contradiction to impress partner. He calls 2 C and *next time*, 4 S.

The third example is not, technically, too strong for a raise to 4 S. But so much of the strength consists in top cards that, if partner has extra values, there may be slam prospects. So on (3), as on (2), it is proper to respond 2 C and to bid 4 S on the next round.

If Opener is only good enough to rebid 2 S, the inferences behind the mechanism of the Delayed Game Raise will be lost. But it will not matter, for then the combined strength of the partnership will not warrant slam ambitions.

The modern tendency is to raise partner's major to game directly on hands rich in distributional values, but to use the Delayed Game Raise on holdings with two or more controls, which offer slam prospects.

The 4-Clubs Convention

Some holdings do not fall conveniently into any existing category. There may be good trump support and two Aces—something to suggest slam possibilities, yet not enough all-round strength to warrant a Delayed Game Raise. To meet this situation a new method has been devised—a response of 4 C over an opening 1 H or 1 S.

The bid is conventional and promises two Aces, and a good fit for partner's major. The 4 C device is still in the experimental stage, but it is destined to gain acceptance, for it has the two prime qualifications for a successful artificial bid: it meets a genuine need; and it is not required in its natural sense. No one decides, there and then, to play a hand in 4 C after partner has opened 1 H or 1 S.

Much the same applies to a direct response of 4 D to one of a major, and this, too, is being tried out as a means of reaching slams which depend more on a combination of distribution and controls than on general high card strength. The 4 D bid is as yet only a blue print, but it may be used already to show good trump support and three Aces—or two Aces and a singleton—according to partnership arrangement. Neither of these weapons—the 4 C or the 4 D jump—is in mass production. Neither has been defined. But both are limited. More powerful hands in support of partner will be discussed later, in Chapter 6.

3

ONE NO TRUMP

The most widely used limit bid is 1 NT. What the limits should be depends on system, convention or special arrangements between partners. But all No Trumps, weak or strong, are narrowly defined. The distribution is always balanced. The three most common patterns are:

4-3-3-3:   4-4-3-2: and 5-3-3-2.

Usually, the 5-card suit is a minor. It may, however, be a very weak major which Opener is not anxious to rebid. Playing a weak NT, this would be an example:

♠ K J 3
♡ 9 7 6 4 2
♢ K 10 4
♣ A Q

In strength the difference between minimum and maximum rarely exceeds 2 points.

In the Acol system, the most popular by far in Britain, the opening 1 NT varies according to vulnerability. Vulnerable, it is strong—16–18. Non-vulnerable, the figure is 13–15, though in neither case is the upper limit often reached in practice by players in the top class.

Responder Takes Charge

A distinctive feature of every sequence which begins with 1 NT is that thereafter most of the decisions are taken by Responder. Sometimes he consults Opener. More often he adds up the two hands and announces the result on his responsibility alone. Since 1 NT is fixed, Responder need only assess his own values to see whether the combined holding warrants a game, slam or part score, or whether the balance of power lies with opponents. When in doubt he can bid 2 NT—or 4 NT—asking partner to go on to game or slam, as the case may be, if he has more than a minimum 1 NT.

Weakness Take Out

On a hand that is poor or even worthless it is proper for Responder to make a *weakness take out* of 1 NT into a suit of five or more cards. This promises no strength whatever and Opener is not expected to bid again.

Opposite 1 NT, weak or strong, Responder calls 2 H on:

	(1)		(2)
♠	3 2		♠	3 2
♡	10 8 7 6 4 2	and	♡	A J 9 8 7
♦	4 3 2		♦	J 10 8 4 2
♣	3 2		♣	3

On (1) he expects to go down regardless of whether the NT is weak or strong. On (2) he should get home without trouble if Opener's is an Acol vulnerable 1 NT. But in both cases 2 H should prove superior to 1 NT.

The bid does not mean: 'Partner I can make 2 H', but rather: 'I don't believe that you can make 1 NT and I think that the hand will play better in Hearts.'

Consulting Opener

Sometimes there is room for doubt. Will it be easier to make game in No Trumps or in a major? Such situations occur when Responder has a fair hand with a 5-card major, but requires further information about a fit. To create a forcing situation, he jumps to 3 H (or 3 S) over 1 NT. With a doubleton, Opener rebids 3 NT, but with three (or four) cards in the major he raises it, usually, to 4, especially if he has a doubleton in another suit.

ONE NO TRUMP

Direct Game Bids

Holding a 6-card major Responder has no need to consult partner and he bids game directly—4 H (or 4 S) over 1 NT. With a long near-solid minor he does best, as a rule, to call 3 NT suppressing his suit altogether. (Compare B and C, p. 33.)

One of the occasions for Opener to re-enter the arena is to give preference when Responder calls two suits. But most of the time his mission is completed with the first bid.

1 NT Always Prepared

Unlike other openings at the One level, 1 NT does not promise a rebid. Subject to the exceptions indicated above, the prospective rebid is: No Bid. And since there is no rebid problem, 1 NT is always prepared.

Tactics

In principle, the handling of the weak No Trump and the strong is identical. Responder allows for a difference of 3 points, and after making the necessary adjustments, adds up and announces the result in the same way, whatever the strength of the 1 NT may be.

Tactical considerations, however, play their part. If Responder knows that Opener is unlikely to have more than 14 he can pass on 10, and sometimes on 11, with impunity. That sets a trap for opponents. If they reopen the bidding, lulled by Responder's pass, they may be badly punished. If they allow 1 NT to stand, they may miss a part score and maybe even a game.

The *trap pass* cannot be exploited in equal measure with the strong NT. Knowing that a 16–18 point hand is against them, opponents will do nothing foolhardy. They are unlikely to miss anything worth while and have little incentive to run risks.

ONE NO TRUMP

1 NT—Openings and Responses

EXAMPLES

Opener

♠ Q 5
♡ K 9 3
◇ K 10 2
♣ A J 4 3 2

Responder

A	B	C
♠ 10 8 6 5 3 2	♠ A J 9 8 7 6 4	♠ A 3
♡ 7	♡ 6	♡ 6
◇ 8 6 3	◇ A 3	◇ A J 9 8 7 6 5
♣ 9 6 5	♣ 9 8 5	♣ 9 8 5

Opener	Responder	Opener	Responder	Opener	Responder
1 NT	2 ♠	1 NT	4 ♠	1 NT	3 NT
No Bid		No Bid		No Bid	

TABLE IV—THE WEAK NO TRUMP

Opener	Count	Responder	Opener's Rebid
1 NT	0–10	No Bid or Weakness Take Out	A weakness Take Out (See *A*) closes the bidding. So does any Game Bid (*B* and *C*).
13–15			
Usual Shape:	11	2 NT	With more than 13, (or *good* 12) call 3 NT.
4–3–3–3 or	12–17	3 NT	Pass *always*.
4–4–3–2 or	18–19	4 NT	With a good 14, call 6 NT but if in doubt, 5 NT.
5–3–3–2	20	6 NT	

If you are playing a STRONG NO TRUMP (16–18), subtract 3 points at every stage in the second column—e.g. bid 2 NT on 8 and 6 NT on 17.

1 No Trump Rebid

A valuable inference brought into play by the weak No Trump lies in the added strength conveyed by the *rebid* of 1 NT.

The pattern is the same in both cases: 4–3–3–3; 4–4–3–2 or 5–3–3–2 with a 5-card minor. If the strength were also the same, there would be no reason to make different bids on identical hands. *All* would be opened 1 NT. It follows that there is room for a variation.

Many of the leading exponents of the weak No Trump limit the bid to 14 points and this allows them to show an extra 1–2 points by opening, say, 1 C and *rebidding* 1 NT.

	(1)	(2)
♠	A 4	4 2
♡	Q 10 9 6	A K Q 2
◇	K 7 4 2	Q J 5
♣	A Q 9	Q J 3 2

(1) Opener calls 1 H and rebids 2 D if Responder calls 2 C. Over 1 S, however, his rebid is 1 NT.

(2) A 1 H opening is not prepared for a 2 D response. The better bid is 1 C. Over 1 D the rebid is 1 H, but over 1 S it is 1 NT. Responder can raise to 3 NT on 11 or on a good 10.

Exchange the Queen of Clubs for a small one and both (1) and (2) would be *opened* 1 NT.

1 No Trump: Weak or Strong?

The price to pay for playing a weak No Trump is the risk of conceding a penalty when most of the outstanding strength is massed in enemy hands. That is why the Acol No Trump varies according to vulnerability. Some Acol players, however, believing that the tactical attractions outweigh the risks, employ a weak No Trump throughout, regardless of vulnerability.

The advantage of opening 1 NT, weak or strong, is that it describes shape and strength in one bid. Also, it has a pre-emptive value. Opponents must enter the auction at the Two level or for ever hold their peace. A drawback is that it may make it difficult for the partnership to find a fit in a major. Opener and Responder may each have four cards in the same major but since Responder does not show a 4-card suit opposite 1 NT, there is a danger of missing good contracts in Spades or Hearts.

The Stayman Convention

To overcome this handicap there exists a convention named after the American master, Sam Stayman. The British variant differs from the original in that it is used more extensively for part score than for game contracts.

The Stayman convention is based on an artificial bid of 2 C by Responder after a 1 NT opening. Partner is asked to bid a 4-card major, if he has one, and 2 D if he has not. It follows that the mechanism must not be set in motion unless Responder is prepared either to end up in a contract of 2 D, 2 S or 2 H, or to make a further bid on the next round.

Opener calls 1 NT and Responder holds:

	(1)		(2)		(3)
♠	10 7 4 2	♠	A J 7 3	♠	10 8 7 3 2
♡	9 8 3 2	♡	3	♡	K J 3 2
◇	8 6 5 4	◇	A K 10 8 3	◇	8 2
♣	7	♣	9 7 2	♣	4 3

Whether the No Trump is weak or strong, there is something to gain each time by applying the Stayman convention.

(1) This is an excellent shape for 2 C. A fit in any one of three suits will lead to a better contract than 1 NT. Even if Opener's only 4-card suit is Clubs, a contract of 2 D may still prove relatively tolerable.

(2) Responder is ready to call 3 NT, but Spades may provide a better spot and it costs nothing to investigate. Unless Opener calls 2 S, Responder will bid 3 NT on the next round.

(3) Hearts will be distinctly superior to No Trumps, if Opener happens to have four Hearts. If he has not, Responder

will call 2 S—which he would have done in the first place, without Stayman.

When Not to Use Stayman

All conventions lend themselves to abuse and this one is no exception. Holding:

	(4)		(5)
♠	10 7 3 2	♠	7 6 5 2
♡	Q 6 4 2	♡	A 10 6
◇	4	◇	A 9 8
♣	A Q J 2	♣	A 9 7

Responder must not bid 2 C on (4), if the weak No Trump is being used. He would be seriously embarrassed by a Response of 2 D.

Opposite a strong No Trump, Stayman is useful here, since Responder is willing to play in 3 NT, but has reason to expect 4 H or 4 S to be superior.

On (5) the convention can serve no purpose. Even if Opener has four Spades it will probably be easier, with this shape, to make 3 NT than 4 S.

The mechanism of what is now generally known as the Stayman convention was devised, in a form somewhat different from the above, by Ewart Kempson in 1933. Today it is in universal use on both sides of the Atlantic—and of the Pacific, too, for that matter.

4

STRONG REBIDS

The same principles apply to Opener's rebids on strong hands as to those that are weak. Only the range is different. Where with 13–15 points the rebid is 1 NT, with 16–18 it is 2 NT. With length in a suit, Opener jumps on the second round to the Three level instead of rebidding his suit at the level of Two. Or else, instead of a simple raise in Responder's suit, he jump raises him from One to Three or from Two to Four.

Minimum Values for Strong Rebids

For a jump rebid in No Trumps over a response at the One level, 17 high card points is about the minimum, and for a double jump (1 H, then 3 NT over 1 S) 19–20.

A balanced 16 point hand may pose an awkward problem, but it is often solved by bidding another suit. This promises no additional strength and partner may pass. If the response is at the Two level, however, Opener rebids 2 NT on 16 and 3 NT on 18. Responder having shown extra values, Opener does not need quite so much himself.

Jump Rebids and Raises in a Suit

For a jump rebid in his suit Opener counts points for length and brings the total to 17 with 15 high card points and a 6-card suit. That is roughly the minimum. In supporting Responder's suit the 3–2–1 scale for shortages comes into operation.

Holding: ♠ A 7 5 2 ♡ A Q J 6 5 3 ◇ 7 ♣ K 4 Opener calls 1 H and jump raises partner's response of 1 S to 3 S.

This example is not quite a minimum for all the high cards

'work'. Each one serves a purpose. Turn the last three cards into ◇ Q and ♣ Q J and the point count would be higher, yet the true value of the cards would be reduced.

Jump Bids Not Forcing

All jump rebids are *limited*. A jump rebid of 2 NT denies the strength to bid 3 NT. A rebid of 3 H, after a 1 H opening, denies the values for 4 H. Therefore, all such bids, though invitational, are not forcing. Responder can pass or he can Sign Off by rebidding his suit at the lowest level as in the sequence

| 1 C | 1 D |
| 2 NT | 3 D |

The 3 D bid indicates a long suit, but no more strength than a pass would do and Opener is not expected to bid again.

Responder Takes Charge

The implications of a Sign Off are the same as those of a weakness take-out after a 1 NT opening. Once again Responder takes charge. He adds the values of the two hands and decides how far the partnership should go. It follows that after a strong rebid, be it in a suit or in No Trumps, Responder should call game or invite a slam on comparatively little. He must bear in mind that if he rebids his suit at the lowest level it is a Sign-Off, the equivalent of a pass.

After the sequence:

Opener	Responder
1 D	1 S
2 NT	

Responder holding:

(1)	(2)	(3)
♠ Q 7 6 5 4 2	♠ Q 10 7 6 3 2	♠ A K 9 7 6 2
♡ 7 6	♡ 7 6	♡ 7
◇ K 4	◇ K 4	◇ K 4 2
♣ 9 8 3	♣ K 8 3	♣ A 8 3

On (1) calls 3 S because, though he may not make it, the hand will surely yield more tricks in Spades than in No Trumps.

On (2) the bid is 4 S, because opposite a strong rebid, Responder can hope to make ten tricks, and if he bids 3 S only, as in (1), Opener will pass.

Similarly, on (3) Responder calls 6 S, because Opener would pass 4 S, which would show a hand like (2).

This quantitative technique, of course, applies to all limit bids.

Jump in a New Suit

As we have seen, a change of suit is not in itself forcing. Partner gives preference, but in doing so—when he likes Opener's second suit best—he may pass. To make certain that the bidding is not dropped when he has a 'rock-crusher', Opener *jumps* in a new suit.

Holding: ♠ K Q 6 ♡ A Q 10 4 2 ◇ A K J 4 ♣ 2, Opener calls 1 H and over 1 S from partner jumps to 3 D. This serves a double purpose. It announces a very big hand and it allows Responder to show a 5-card Spade suit, if he has one, or to give preference in Hearts on the slenderest values. Responder should not bid 3 NT if he has nothing in Clubs. But he must say something. He cannot pass.

STRONG REBIDS

Strength-Showing Rebids by Opener

EXAMPLES

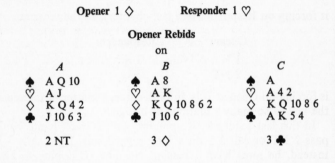

Opener 1 ◊   Responder 1 ♡

Opener Rebids
on

A	B	C
♠ A Q 10	♠ A 8	♠ A
♡ A J	♡ A K	♡ A 4 2
◊ K Q 4 2	◊ K Q 10 8 6 2	◊ K Q 10 8 6
♣ J 10 6 3	♣ J 10 6	♣ A K 5 4
2 NT	3 ◊	3 ♣

TABLE V

Opening Sequence		Opener's Rebids		
Op.	Res.	Count 17–18	Count 19–20	
1 D	1 H	2 NT	3 NT	Balanced hand and no unguarded suit.
		3 D	—	Usually a 6-card suit.
		3 H	4 H	At least four Hearts.
		New suit	Jump in a new suit	A jump consists in bidding *one more* than is necessary to over-call the previous bid (see *C*).

When a Change of Suit is Forcing

In certain situations a change of suit is forcing *by inference* and though a jump shift may be made for other reasons, it is no longer essential as a means of keeping the bidding open.

Just as the sequence

Opener	Responder
1 H	2 NT
3 D	

is forcing on Responder (see last chapter), so the sequence

Opener	Responder
1 H	1 S
2 NT	3 D

is forcing on Opener. It is, in both cases, a matter of inference, the key to so many situations at bridge.

In this last sequence, Responder, with a weak hand, could pass 2 NT or call 3 S on a long ragged suit. If he calls 3 D instead, he must have a reason. He may be hoping to hear delayed Spade support from partner. Or he may have a two-suiter in Spades and Diamonds. Or he may be waiting to see if Opener can rebid Hearts. On the face of it, Responder is looking for an alternative to 3 NT, but he clearly wants to be in game.

Similarly, the sequence

Opener	Responder
1 H	1 S
2 NT	3 H

is unconditionally forcing. It indicates that Responder, with three Hearts—having four he would have raised the suit at once—is suggesting 4 H as an alternative to 3 NT. If Opener has four Hearts only, there is a chance that he may be able to call 3 S and if Responder has five, the contract will be 4 S.

Follow the next sequence to the end:

Opener	Responder
♠ J 4 2	♠ K Q 9 5 4
♡ A 10 3	♡ 7
◇ K Q 5	◇ A J 6 2
♣ A K 6 3	♣ 7 5 2

41

Bidding

1 C	1 S
2 NT	3 D
3 S	4 S

It is easy to make 4 S, and probably 5 S, but 3 NT may go two down on a Heart lead. Yet give Opener: ♠ 4 2 ♡ K Q 10 ◇ Q 4 2 ♣ A K Q 6 3 and 3 NT is the better contract.

A Two-Suiter

With a two-suiter Responder rebids the second suit, not the first. The inference is that *both* suits are rebiddable. It is assumed that the shorter suit was not opened before the longer. If, therefore, the second suit can be rebid, this must apply in equal measure to the first suit.

Here is a typical situation:

Opener	**Responder**
♠ A 7	♠ K J 7 3 2
♡ K 3 2	♡ A 10 9 4 2
◇ A Q J 10 4	◇ 7 3
♣ K 9 6	♣ 5

Bidding

1 D	1 S
2 NT	3 H
3 NT	4 H
No Bid	

Opener does not raise Hearts the first time, for partner may have no more than four—just as Responder had four Diamonds only in the previous example.

Forcing or Not Forcing?

There must never be a doubt in a player's mind as to whether a change of suit is or is not forcing. Above all, there must be no confusion between delayed support for partner's suit and a Sign-Off. The distinction is unmistakable.

A Sign-Off consists in rebidding the *same suit* at the lowest level. If it is not the same suit as on the previous round, then it is not a Sign-Off.

A change of suit at the level of One or Two is not forcing. But it is *nearly always* forcing at the Three level, especially after a strength showing rebid like 2 NT.

Trial Bids

Once a fit in a major has been established it becomes the *agreed suit*. The bid of a new suit at this stage is not an attempt to find a better contract, but an invitation to partner to bid game if he has a little to spare.

After sequences such as:

$$1 S — 2 S \quad \text{or} \quad \begin{array}{c} 1 C — 1 H \\ 2 H \end{array}$$

a bid in any new suit is a *trial bid*, showing additional strength, urging partner to go on and directing his attention to the new suit. With K x he writes up the value of his hand. With x x x he writes it down.

A trial bid—in a suit, though not in No Trumps—is unconditionally forcing at any level and must never be passed. In the above sequence of 1 S—2 S, Opener may have:

(1)	(2)	(3)
♠ A Q 7 4 2	♠ A Q 7 4	♠ K Q 10 6 4 2
♡ A K	♡ A K 6	♡ 7 6
◇ K 4 3 2	◇ Q 4 2	◇ A J 9 6
♣ 8 6	♣ Q 10 6	♣ 3

He bids 3 D on (1), hoping that if Responder can stretch a little, and especially if he has a useful feature in Diamonds, he will bid 4 S.

On (2) Opener rebids 2 NT, which is *not* forcing, though it shows a good hand and is an invitation.

STRONG REBIDS

Pre-emptive Raise

On (3) the best bid is 3 S. This used to be played as a strength-showing bid, but is so no longer. It is a barrage bid, intended to prevent opponents from coming in. Opener can see that if all partner can do is call 2 S his side is unlikely to muster four defensive tricks against 4 H. Hence his 3 S. This is *not* a trial bid and Responder is not expected to bid again, even on a maximum.

Trial Bids by Responder

Opener and Responder are in the same position. Either can make a trial bid or call one more, pre-emptively, after a simple raise, as in (3) above.

After the sequence:

Opener	Responder
1 C	1 S
2 S	

Responder holding:

(a)	(b)
♠ K 9 6 3 2	♠ K 9 5 4 3 2
♡ K 10 4 2	♡ 7
◇ 10 8	◇ 8 4 2
♣ A 7	♣ Q J 10

(a) calls 3 Hearts, hoping that Opener can find 4 S.

(b) calls 3 S to raise a barrage against opponents, who must have appreciable values on the bidding and may enter the auction if Responder passes.

5

REVERSES

In few situations at bridge is strength revealed through inference so unmistakably as in Reverse sequences. Compare the following:

Opener	Responder		Opener	Responder
(1)		and (2)		
1 S	2 D		1 H	2 D
2 H			2 S	

In the first case, with a minimum for his 2 D bid, Responder can show preference at the Two level, passing if he prefers Hearts and putting Opener back to 2 Spades, if he does not.

By contrast, in the second case, Responder can only show preference for Hearts by making a bid at the *level of Three*. Opener, by the order in which he bid his two suits, put partner in that position. To have done so, he needed a strong hand. That is the inference.

This sequence, in which the lower ranking of two touching suits is bid first and the higher ranking one next, is known as a *reverse*. It has two distinctive features:

1. The first (lower ranking suit) is *always* longer than the second.

2. The hand must be strong enough to stand preference from partner at the Three level, even if his original response was made on the barest minimum. That means some 17 high card points on 5–4–2–2—the least favourable distribution for a reverse. This may be shaded, principally:

(a) if the shape is 5–4–3–1 with the three cards in Responder's suit.

45

(b) if Opener has a 6-card suit, or better still, one 6-card and one 5-card suit.

Raising the Level

Certain rebids have some of the implications of a full-blooded Reverse, but not all, as in the sequence:

Opener	Responder
1 D	2 C
2 S	

Since Opener must be prepared for preference at the Three level, he must be strong. But since the suits are not touching there is no guarantee that the Diamonds are longer than the Spades. The suits may be of equal length.

Expecting Responder to bid 1 H, Opener calls 1 D on:

♠ Q 10 7 6 2 ♡ — ◇ A Q J 10 9 ♣ A K 3. Over 2 C, however, he bids 2 S. The response has materially improved his holding.

Or again with: ♠ 6 ♡ A K 10 4 2 ◇ K 3 ♣ A Q J 7 6 the opening is 1 H and the rebid over 2 D is 3 C. Certainly opener must be strong, but he may or may not have longer Hearts than Clubs.

Responding to Opener's Reverse

Turn to Responder. Opener called 1 H, then, over 2 D, he bid 2 S, a typical Reverse.

Responder holds:

(1)	(2)	(3)
♠ 4 2	♠ Q 4 3 2	♠ Q 2
♡ 4 3 2	♡ 4 3	♡ K 10 2
◇ A K Q 10 8	◇ A K Q 10 8	◇ A 9 8 3 2
♣ 10 6 3	♣ 7 6	♣ 4 3 2

On (1) he bids 3 H, mere preference. He knows that Opener must be strong, precisely because he put him into the position of having to make so high a bid on so modest a hand. And he must have not less than five Hearts.

(2) The bid is 4 S—not just 3 S, which would have been enough if the Spades were 5 4 3 2. With the ♠ Q the hand is worth a jump raise.

(3) 4 H. Though the point count is the same as in (1), it is a far better fit and every high card *works*.

(4)	(5)	(6)
♠ 4 2	♠ Q 4	♠ Q J 3
♡ 7 6	♡ Q J	♡ Q J
◇ A K J 10 8	◇ A 8 7 6 2	◇ A 8 7 6 2
♣ J 10 4 2	♣ J 10 4 2	♣ 4 3 2

(4) 2 NT. Despite the combined count, which should suffice for game, there is real danger of a misfit.

(5) 3 NT—with complete confidence, for the honours in the majors promise to give solidity to partner's suits.

(6) 4 H. A doubleton will do opposite a 5-card (or 6-card) suit. In Spades the hand will not play well if Opener is forced early in Clubs.

REVERSES

Opener's Reverse Sequence

EXAMPLES

Opener

♠ A K 10 4 2
♡ A K J 7 6 3
♢ 2
♣ 2

Responder

	A		B		C
♠	7 6 3	♠	Q 6	♠	Q 5
♡	10 4	♡	10 4	♡	Q 5
♢	K J 10 7 6	♢	K 9 8 7 6	♢	A 10 6 5 3
♣	A J 9	♣	A 10 4 3	♣	K Q 9 6

Opener	Responder	Opener	Responder	Opener	Responder
1 ♡	2 ♢	1 ♡	2 ♢	1 ♡	2 ♢
2 ♠	2 NT	2 ♠	2 NT	2 ♠	3 ♣
3 ♠	4 ♠	3 ♠	4 ♡	3 ♠	6 ♡

TABLE VI

Opening Sequence	Shape	High Card Count	General Considerations
1 H 2 C 2 S	♠♡♢♣ 4–5–2–2	17	With tops in the long suits and no wasted strength in Diamonds, shade to 16.
	4–5–1–3	16	The minimum is reduced slightly on account of the fit in Clubs.
	4–6–1–2	15	Singleton honours, except Aces, do not count.
	5–6–1–1	14	
	5–6–0–2	13	Note that the void is in Diamonds, not in Responder's suit, Clubs.

With five Spades, six Hearts and less than 13 high card points, open 1 S, then bid *and rebid* Hearts.

48

REVERSES

Reverses by Responder

Like Opener, Responder initiates, at times, a reverse sequence and the implications are the same. His first suit is longer than his second and he is strong enough to stand preference at the Three level, which means, in effect, that his count is 11 or so.

Minimum Values

Over Opener's 1 D Responder calls 1 H, and over a rebid of 2 D he bids 2 S. The barest minimum for this sequence would be:

♠ A K 4 2
♡ A 9 7 6 3
♢ 4 2
♣ 10 3

Responder has the high card values for 2 NT, but he has no guard in Clubs. Besides, 2 S is more informative, because:

(a) it shows, by inference, five Hearts. For Responder, as for Opener, the same rule applies: if the lower ranking of two touching suits is bid first and the higher ranking suit next, the first must *always* be longer than the second.

(b) Opener may have what he considers an 'unbiddable' Spade suit, and if so, 4 S may be the right contract. Or else, Opener may prefer to play the hand in No Trumps, but has no guard in Spades.

Observe that if Opener rebids 2 NT, Responder should pass. He had bid his hand to the full, when he reversed, and there is nothing left for him to say.

With: ♠ 10 9 2 ♡ 8 3 ♢ K Q J 10 4 ♣ A K 6 Opener should bid 3 NT. He can see six playing tricks and Responder's sequence indicates that he will find three, at least, in dummy.

A Warning on Reverses

So much mumbo-jumbo, hearsay and even superstition,

centre on reverses, that the subject calls for a word of warning. A reverse is a sequence. It is not a system or a convention. It is a natural development of the hand and has no hidden meaning. The sequence shows strength, because it is a luxury in terms of bidding space. Instead of keeping the bidding low, it pushes it higher. So long as you have foreseen the next move and can stand preference from partner at the Three level, even if he is very weak, you can reverse with an easy conscience. The 17 and 11 requirements for Opener and Responder respectively are only guiding principles. They are not all important—like looking ahead to the next move.

6

FORCING TAKE OUT
(or JUMP SHIFT)

No Responder in the preceding pages has held more than 15–16 high card points or the distributional equivalent. That is the maximum for a Delayed Game Raise—a sequence designed to show a big, but none the less limited, hand.

What happens if Responder has 18–20 or even more? The answer is a Forcing Take Out or Jump Shift (the more logical American term), a first round jump in a new suit. This is generally known as a Force, though the term is apt to be misleading, since no first round response in a new suit can be passed anyway. The difference is that a Jump Shift is forcing, not just for one round, but till *game is reached*.

It is an unlimited bid, which has a minimum, but no maximum. A first round force does not always promise a good suit or a fit for partner's, but without one or the other, Responder needs to be correspondingly stronger.

Qualifications for a Force

The general practice is to Force with a good 16 *nearly always*, and sometimes with appreciably less. Apart from all-round strength, there are three important elements: a solid suit; an outstanding fit for partner's; and controls—Aces, voids, and on occasion, even a singleton. A combination of any two of these factors generally calls for a Jump Shift.

As soon as a slam comes into the line of vision, controls acquire a special virtue. Three Aces or two Aces and a singleton, added to a fit for partner's suit, are worth far more than their face value in points.

Before examining more closely the qualifications for a Force, consider the question: Why Force in the first place? The answer is that unless an outsize hand is shown at once it is often difficult or impossible to catch up later.

Reasons for Forcing

Partner opens 1 C and you hold:

♠ A J 7 6 5 ♡ A K Q ◇ 3 2 ♣ A 3 2. If you respond 1 S, what reasonable bid can you make on the next round over 2 C or 1 NT—or anything else, for that matter? The same problem is posed by the next three hands, though each one differs structurally from the other two.

Opener calls 1 H and Responder holds:

	(1)	(2)	(3)
♠	A K 10 7	A Q 4	A K Q J 9 7
♡	4 2	K 10 9 8 4 3 2	—
◇	A K Q	—	A Q 3
♣	9 8 6 2	K 3 2	J 8 4 3

(1) The best bid is 2 S and the intended rebid is 3 NT (over 3 H) or 4 S (over 3 S). This is a minimum Force, based on high cards alone. But 1 S is not enough. Partner must be roused.

(2) 3 C. The sensational fit in Hearts demands a dramatic gesture. Observe that a jump in a *lower ranking* 3-card suit presents no danger. No matter how much partner may raise Clubs, you can always go back to Hearts at the *same level*.

(3) 2 S. Controls and a solid suit more than make up for the void in partner's Hearts.

Opener's Rebid after Jump Shift

In response to a first round Force, Opener makes his *natural rebid*. If he opened 1 H, intending to rebid 2 H, he will now call 3 H over, say, 2 S or 3 D. And if his opening was 1 C, and the intended rebid was 1 NT, over 2 H he will rebid 2 NT.

Once upon a time, a rebid in No Trumps, after a Force, was a conventional Sign-Off. This crude method has been discarded from modern bidding in favour of the *natural rebid*. In some cases, a rebid in No Trumps would show strength, as in the sequence.

Opener	Responder
1 S	3 C
3 NT	

Why should this show strength? Because Opener's intended rebid over 2 C would have been, presumably, 2 NT. This would have shown a balanced hand with some 16 points. Since Opener must now find a rebid at the level of Three, he is still showing the same values.

This implies, of course, that Opener must not alter the pre-destined course of the auction on account of the Force. He must make precisely the same rebid—at the higher level forced upon him by the Jump.

Normal Trump Support

It is generally unwise to Force on a flimsy suit, but at times it is unavoidable. Bearing this in mind, Opener should not strain to raise his partner on 3-card support.

Opener calls 1 C and Responder Forces with 2 H.

Opener holds:

(1)	(2)	(3)
♠ K 10 3 2	♠ A 4	♠ Q J 4
♡ A Q 9	♡ 8 7 6 2	♡ K J 4
♢ 7 3	♢ 7 3	♢ K Q J
♣ A 10 7 6	♣ A K J 6 3	♣ A 9 8 2

(1) Opener's rebid is 2 S, since over 1 H he intended to bid 1 S. The Heart support can be shown later.

(2) 3 H. Again the natural rebid. Enrich the hand with an Ace and a Heart honour, and the bid would still be 3 H. The additional values would be shown afterwards. One of the advantages of a first round Force is to ensure that there will be plenty of room for 'afterwards'.

(3) 3 NT. The intended rebid was a jump to 2 NT. The Opener must still jump, but he can no longer do it under the level of Three.

The Modern Trend

Experience shows that on big hands a Jump Shift allows more room for Slam investigation. The modern tendency, therefore, is to Force more lightly than was the custom in former years—especially on distributional hands. It keeps the bidding *lower*.

A Warning

The theme of the Forcing Take Out or Jump Shift cannot be brought to a close without a warning.

Only a *single jump* (2 H over 1 D) shows strength. A double jump (3 H over 1 D) is the opposite—a weak bid, based on a long, broken suit, and is intended to shut out opponents.

A treble jump (4 H over 1 D) is not quite so weak, but it is still far from strong. Shut out or pre-emptive bids will be studied in a later chapter. Meanwhile, let it be noted that only a *single jump* compels partner to bid again. Over a double or treble jump he is expected to pass, unless he is exceptionally strong.

7

SLAM BIDDING

Even experienced players may be guided by this rough and ready rule: when partner opens the bidding and you are good enough to open yourself, you have enough between you to be in game. And when partner announces the values for a strong rebid (or a strong 1 NT opening) and you have similar values, you are in the slam zone.

The arithmetic is simple. An opening bid presupposes 13 points. The minimum for a strong rebid is 16–17. Subject to a misfit, 26 points between the two hands suffice for game and anything over 32 must encourage slam ambitions.

If partner opens 1 NT, weak (13–14), and you have 20 high card points, you can call 6 NT directly. The same applies if you have 14, and partner, having opened 1 C, rebids 3 NT over a response from you at the One level. At worst the slam will be on a finesse.

Controls

But it is not always as easy as that. To make a slam it is not enough to have the all-round strength to win twelve tricks. If controls are lacking opponents may take the first two.

Partner opens 1 C and you hold:

♠ A 7 2   ♡ A K Q J 10   ◇ 2   ♣ K Q J 10

You can see more than thirteen tricks, yet you will fail to make twelve if partner is Aceless, and he could have opened on:

♠ K Q J   ♡ —   ◇ K Q J 10   ♣ 9 8 7 6 4 2

It comes down to a question of controls. If partner has two

Aces you can be pretty certain of a Grand Slam. If he has none you must not go beyond 5 C.

Blackwood

Various conventions have been devised to meet this situation, but by far the simplest and the most popular is Blackwood, which functions like this:

When a suit has been agreed, *though not otherwise*, a call of 4 NT is conventional and asks partner to show how many Aces he has.

With no Ace he responds 5 C. With one Ace the bid is 5 D, with two 5 H and with three 5 S. One suit up for every Ace.

If a Grand Slam is envisaged the same procedure can be repeated with a bid of 5 NT to ask for Kings.

Some tournament pairs use the 5 C response to 4 NT to show all four Aces, as well as no Ace. On the face of it the gulf is so wide that there should be no misunderstanding. In practice, however, even experts have been known to go wrong and for general purposes it is best to ignore this variation altogether.

Blackwood and the Minors

At all times Blackwood should be used sparingly. Its purpose is not so much to pave the way for good slams as to discourage bad ones. Blackwood should be largely confined to hands of a certain type, where only Aces matter. And great care should be exercised before invoking the convention when the agreed suit is a minor, especially Clubs.

This would be a hand made for Blackwood. Partner bids 1 H and you hold:

♠ A K Q 4 3 2   ♡ K Q J 6 5   ◇ J   ♣ Q

You call 4 NT and if partner shows three Aces (5 S) you will bid 7 H. If he has two (5 H) you will stop in a small slam, and if he has only one you will still be safe in 5 H.

But if the agreed suit is Clubs, instead of Hearts, Blackwood cannot be applied, for to show one Ace partner would have to call 5 D and you would land in 6 C knowing in advance that opponents could take the first two tricks.

Showing a Void

To show a void is never easy and always calls for good partnership understanding. The Blackwood convention does not lend itself to it readily, but several methods have been devised. The simplest allows Responder to 4 NT to jump the level in showing his Aces. With one Ace and a void the response is not 5 Diamonds, but 6 Diamonds. With two Aces it is 6 Hearts. Since the response is at the small slam level, the void cannot be shown unless a Grand Slam is envisaged.

Only very experienced partnerships should apply this part of Blackwood.

Gerber

A variant of the Blackwood Convention has been devised by the American player, J. Gerber for use opposite an opening of 1 No Trump or 2 No Trumps.

The enquiry for Aces takes the form of 4 Clubs. Partner replies step by step. Without an Ace, he calls 4 Diamonds. With one Ace, the bid is 4 Hearts, with two, 4 Spades and with three Aces, 4 No Trumps. A 5 Clubs response shows all four Aces.

```
        ♠ K 3
        ♡ J 2
        ◇ K Q 9 8 7 5 3
        ♣ K 2
            N
        W       E
            S
        ♠ A Q 7 2
        ♡ A 4 3
        ◇ A 4 2
        ♣ A Q J
```

South	North
2 NT	4 C
5 C	7 NT

Had South shown three Aces only by bidding 4 No Trumps, the contract would have been 6 No Trumps.

The Gerber convention can be used in a variety of ways, but is at its best opposite No Trump openings and few players employ it at any other time.

Quantitative 4 No Trumps

There are occasions when 4 NT is a straightforward, quantitative bid, as after partner's 1 NT opening or after a strength showing rebid by him of 2 or 3 NT. This should never be confused with Blackwood or with any other convention.

Blackwood comes into operation only after a suit has been agreed. When the previous bid was in No Trumps, any 4 NT bid is quantitative and may be passed.

There is one exception to this. After a Forcing Take Out it is usual to treat 4 NT as conventional.

In the sequence:

Opener	Responder		Opener	Responder
1 S	2 NT		1 H	2 D
4 NT		or	3 NT	4 NT

the bid is quantitative,   but in

Opener	Responder		Opener	Responder
1 S	3 H		1 NT	3 D
4 C	4 H	or	3 NT	4 NT
4 NT				

it is conventional. The assumption is that the player who bids 4 NT knows in which denomination the hand will be played—his own suit or partner's, or maybe in No Trumps. After a Force, a suit may be agreed by implication.

Slam Tries

Most slams do not lend themselves to direct quantitative

methods and Blackwood does not always give the answer to the problem of controls.

When the bidding indicates that there is enough all-round strength for a slam, partner must be taken into consultation. It is not enough to put blunt questions to him, such as 'How many Aces have you?' He must be invited to co-operate more fully than that.

The first step is a Trial Bid. This closely follows the pattern of the trial bids discussed in Chapter 4. The difference is that the level is higher and the objective is no longer a game, but a slam.

Once a major has been agreed any bid in a new suit, which takes the auction to the game level or beyond, is a *slam try*. If partner does not want to accept the invitation he signs off in the agreed suit. A bid by him in any other suit is encouraging. And since interest, when the partnership enters the slam zone, centres largely on controls, the response to a trial bid shows, not a secondary suit, but a feature—an Ace, a singleton, or possibly a void. This is known as a Cue Bid.

Cue Bids

Opener bids 1 H on:

♠ A 6   ♡ A 10 8 7 6 4   ◇ 6   ♣ A Q J 5

Responder raises to 3 H. This puts the partnership in the slam zone, but the future is still uncertain and Opener consults his partner with 4 C, a slam try.

Responder may have:

(1)	(2)	(3)
♠ K J 8 7	♠ Q J 7 3	♠ K 8 7
♡ Q J 5 2	♡ Q 9 5 3	♡ K Q 9 5
◇ A 7 3	◇ A J	◇ 9 8 4 2
♣ 8 6	♣ 7 6 2	♣ K 3

On (1) Responder calls 4 D. Having full values for his raise to 3 H he has no reason to decline Opener's invitation and he shows his principal feature, the D Ace.

On (2) 4 H, a sign off. The Ace of Diamonds is still there, but the rest of the hand is not encouraging. The Q J combination in a side suit is a dubious asset in a slam and the three small Clubs, the suit in which partner made his slam try, is also a deterrent.

(3) 5 C. There is no Ace to show, but other values more than make up for it. Partner will not misunderstand. If the D Ace is vital to him, he will stop in 5 H. If the C K and good trump support suffice, he will bid the slam.

He knows, of course, that if Responder had an Ace he would show it in preference to bidding 5 C, for it is part of the technique of cue bidding that an Ace should be shown before a King.

Slam Try by Responder

Responder is as likely as his partner to make a slam try. Opener calls 1 C and raises Responder's 1 S to 4 S. With:

♠ K Q 7 6 3 2   ♡ 7   ◇ J 4   ♣ A J 9 3

Responder has reason to be optimistic. Yet Opener might have as much as:

♠ A J 10 4   ♡ A K   ◇ Q 3   ♣ K Q 10 6 2

and still opponents could win the first two tricks with the Ace and King of Diamonds.

To investigate, Responder calls 5 C, inviting a cue bid. If Opener calls 5 D, he bids the slam. If it is 5 H, he stops in 5 S. The usual practice with two Aces is to bid the lower ranking one first, so that 5 H almost certainly denies the Ace of Diamonds.

Over 5 S, Opener, with a singleton Diamond or the K Q, can still bid the slam. Again it is a matter of inference. If Responder made a slam try, but lost interest after hearing about the Ace of Hearts, he must be preoccupied with Diamonds.

SLAM BIDDING

The essence of cue bidding is to pinpoint the controls, for one Ace is not always as good as another.

Inferential Cue Bid

The opening is 1 NT (weak) on:

♠ 3 2
♡ A Q 4 2
◇ K 8 6
♣ A 7 6 5

and partner bids 3 H. The general practice in this situation, as we saw in Chapter 3, is to raise to 4 H on three (or four) prospective trumps. But it costs nothing to call 4 C, showing the Ace, and by inference, a hand suitable for a slam. Responder knows the limits of his partner's strength and he can close the bidding with 4 H, if his values do not justify slam aspirations.

But the cards could have been dealt like this:

Opener	Responder
♠ 3 2	♠ A Q
♡ A Q 4 2	♡ K 10 8 6 5
◇ K 8 6	◇ A Q 4 2
♣ A 7 6 5	♣ K Q

Bidding

1 NT	3 H
4 C	4 D
5 H	5 S
6 D	7 H

Responder confirms that he was looking for a slam by cue-bidding the D Ace. Opener's jump in Hearts shows exceptional trump support and Responder's 5 S is a Grand Slam inquiry. Unless Spades is the agreed suit, a bid of 5 S is *always* a Grand Slam try, for by then the partnership is committed to the Six level, anyway. If there were no hope of reaching Seven, the small slam would be bid directly, without further ado.

61

Over 5 S Opener can almost bid 7 H, but again it costs nothing to show the King of Diamonds. That completes a picture of his hand, for the C Ace and the two honours in Hearts have been shown already. Responder will then be put in possession of all the information before deciding whether or not to call the Grand Slam.

Cue Bidding a Void

Like an Ace, a void is a first round control and on freak distributional hands it can be just as valuable.

Opener	Responder
♠ A Q	♠ K 9 8 7 5 4 3 2
♡ A K Q 9 8 2	♡ 6
◇ A K 6	◇ —
♣ J 4	♣ K Q 8 3

Bidding

2 C	2 S
3 H	3 S
5 S	

Clearly the Grand Slam depends on finding Opener with the C Ace. To find out, Responder shows his only control—the void in Diamonds. If Opener has the Ace of Diamonds he will be alive to the duplication of values and he will break hard. If he has not, he will bid the Grand Slam for all four controls will have been located.

The Grand Slam Force

A well-known convention, which has a place in this chapter, is the Grand Slam Force. Opportunities for using it come up rarely, but when they do, the convention is invaluable.

Partner opens 1 S and you hold:

♠ K 9 3 2
♡ —
◇ A K Q 7 6 5 3
♣ A 6

You do not want to know whether partner is good or bad. You are only concerned with two specific cards, the Ace and the Queen of Spades. To inquire about them you bid 5 NT. This asks partner to call Seven if he has *two of the three top honours* of the agreed suit. If he has not, he calls Six. Often, of course, as in the above example, the suit is agreed by implication.

The Grand Slam Force can never be mistaken for the Blackwood inquiry for Kings. The latter comes into force only *after* the 4 NT bid has been used. The Grand Slam Force is bid directly, without being preceded by 4 NT.

8

TWO BIDS

An opening Two Bid announces a hand of exceptional strength and calls on Responder to keep open the bidding, whatever his holding.

In the early days of Contract, during the Culbertson era, a Two Bid in any suit was forcing on partner to game. This convention has been largely superseded by 2 Clubs as the recognized Game Demand Bid. A distinctive feature of all 2 Club systems—Acol, though the most important, is only one of several—is the Intermediate Two Bid in the other three suits. This shows near-game values on distributional hands, which are difficult to describe in the ordinary way.

Holdings in both categories, game and near-game, may be balanced or unbalanced. The former, whatever their strength, conform closely to the No Trump pattern. The latter call for special treatment and will be studied separately.

Super No Trumps

The biggest balanced hands differ only in size from their smaller brethren—the weak No Trump, the strong No Trump and the jump No Trump rebids. The shape is the same, but the range of these super No Trump hands extends beyond the 19–20 group. The procedure is as before. Responder adds his values to partner's and more often than not announces the final contract on the first round.

Table VII shows three stages in the super No Trump group, each stage 2 points ahead of the one before, extending all the way from 21 to 26 and beyond. And in each of the three categories the margin between minimum and maximum is only 1 point—21–22, 23–24, 25–26.

TWO BIDS

The Acol 2 C Variant

Worthy of note is the specialized Acol 2 Clubs opening, *followed by a rebid of 2 NT*. This provides the sole exception to the rule that a 2 C bid must be kept open unconditionally till game is reached. The 2 NT rebid shows a count of 23–24, which is not quite enough for game, and on a worthless hand Responder may pass. With 25–26 Opener rebids 3 NT. Needless to say, partner needs very little to invite a slam, but if he simply calls 4 H or 4 S, he shows length without strength, making the equivalent at game level of a weakness take out.

Even more powerful hands—with 27 or more points—come up from time to time. But this is rare and there is no universally accepted procedure in such situations.

The 3 C Convention

Just as the Stayman convention helps to find a major suit fit after a 1 NT opening, so another device, an artificial bid of 3 C over 2 NT sometimes leads to a slam which depends on a 4–4 fit in trumps.

The 3 C bid asks Opener to show his 4-card suit, and if he has two suits, minor or major, to bid them in ascending order. It follows that if Opener replies 3 S, he cannot have any other 4-card suit. With Clubs as the only 4-card suit the rebid is 3 NT.

This is how the convention works:

Opener	Responder
♠ A 8 6	♠ J 4 2
♡ K J 2	♡ A Q 9 4
◇ A Q 7 3	◇ K J 4 3
♣ A K 3	♣ 4 2

Bidding

2 NT	3 C
3 D	6 D

In No Trumps the limit is eleven tricks, which is the normal expectation with 32 points. With a 4–4 fit in a suit an extra trick materializes, which again conforms to expectations. Opener discards a Spade on dummy's long Heart and makes the twelfth trick by ruffing a Spade in his hand. Or else he ruffs a club in dummy.

If no 4–4 fit is brought to light, Responder can still bid 4 NT, a quantitative bid inviting Opener to call a Slam if he has anything over a minimum.

Baron 2 No Trumps

Some of Britain's leading players keep their opening 1 NT within the narrow limits of 13 to 14 or rather between a *good* 12 and a *poor* 14. No longer needed as a natural bid, 2 NT over 1 NT is reserved for purposes of slam investigation. Opener bids his suit or suits in ascending order in the same way as after the artificial 3 Clubs response to 2 NT.

This convention is named after Leo Baron whose team had a run of brilliant successes in the immediate post-war years.

A Major over 2 NT

With a 5- or 6-card major and a void or singleton in his hand, Responder may look for a suit contract in preference to No Trumps. Opener will usually raise the major on 3-card support. With a doubleton he will rebid 3 NT.

Having a maximum and a good fit for Responder, Opener should make a cue-bid—e.g. 4 D over 3 S—as a slam try. If Responder declines the invitation and rebids his major—which has been agreed by inference—Opener will have no more to say. But the cue-bid costs nothing for it does not raise the level and it cannot mislead Responder, who knows the limits of his partner's strength.

Flint Transfer Bid

Lack of bidding space does not permit a weakness take out of 2 NT. Jeremy Flint, one of our younger stars, and a member of Britain's team in the world championship of 1965 at Buenos Aires, has devised a partial substitute which Responder may use when he holds a trickless hand with a long major, like:

♠ x x ♡ J x x x x x ◇ x x ♣ x x x.

Over an opening 2 NT he calls an artificial 3 D. Opener replies 3 H *automatically*. If Responder's suit is Hearts, he passes. If it is the other major, he calls 3 S and Opener passes.

This is not for general use, but in tournament bridge the Flint convention has proved its worth.

3 NT Opening

Going back to the days of Culbertson's Forcing Two, there are still players today who open 3 NT on balanced 25–26 point hands. That is a wasteful practice, for such hands are well described by an opening 2 C followed by a rebid of 3 NT.

An opening 3 NT belongs logically to a different distributional group. In modern bridge this bid is made not on a balanced pattern, but on a long solid minor with a few honour cards outside. There may be a singleton, perhaps even an unguarded suit, for the bid is speculative, and after partner has passed, it may contain an element of bluff.

Open 3 NT on:

(1)	(2)	(3)
♠ Q J 2	♠ 4 2	♠ K 2
♡ K 2	♡ A	♡ K 2
◇ A K Q J 7 6 2	◇ K 10 4	◇ K 2
♣ K	♣ A K Q 8 6 4 2	♣ A K Q J 4 3 2

The last is the classical example since it is an obvious advantage to have the opening lead run up to the Kings. But all three hands are legitimate 3 NT openings.

Big Distributional Hands

All 2 Club systems distinguish between game and near-game hands, the unlimited and the limited. For the latter the Acol model is now in almost universal use. It is based on eight playing tricks and a good suit, usually a 6-card suit. Or else it is a two-suited hand. The Intermediate Two Bid is not measured in points, though the count is unlikely to fall below 16 and is usually higher. Apart from playing tricks, there must be controls and high cards in at least two suits, as in:

	(1)	(2)	(3)
♠	A K Q J 8 6	A 2	K Q J 10 6 2
♡	A J 6 4	A K J 10 6 5	A
◇	K Q	K Q J	A Q 9 7 3
♣	2	3 2	2

In each case the hand will prove unmanageable if it is opened with a One bid. Partner should be told at once that a game is nearly certain and that if he has anything worth while, a slam may be round the corner.

But . . .

	(1)	(2)	(3)
♠	—	A K Q J	A K Q J 7 6
♡	A K Q J 6 5 4 2	A K Q J	A K Q
◇	Q 4 2	10 4 2	A 2
♣	J 3	3 2	3 2

None of the above is cast in the mould of an Intermediate Two Bid, though each example has at least eight playing tricks.

On (1) 4 H is the best bid, compelling opponents to start guessing at the ten-trick level.

(2) A Two Bid is *never* made on a 4-card suit.

(3) This is *too good*. The combination of playing tricks and controls puts the hand in the unlimited category and demands nothing less than a Game Demand Bid—2 C, *followed by 2 S*, which is, of course, unconditionally forcing to game.

TWO BIDS

Super No Trumps Range (Acol)

Opener

A	B	C
♠ A J 2	♠ A K J	♠ A K 2
♡ A Q 7	♡ A Q 7	♡ A Q 7
◇ K J 4	◇ K J 4	◇ K Q 4
♣ A Q 8 2	♣ A Q 8 2	♣ A Q J 8

Responder (i)

♠ Q 4
♡ K 10 8 4 2
◇ A 5 3
♣ 5 4 3

A		B		C	
Opener	*Responder*	*Opener*	*Responder*	*Opener*	*Responder*
2 NT	3 NT	2 ♣	2 ♡	2 ♣	2 ♡
No Bid		2 NT	4 NT	3 NT	6 NT
		6 NT			

Responder (ii)

♠ 9 8 7 6 5 4 3
♡ J 6
◇ 3 2
♣ J 3

D		E		F	
Opener	*Responder*	*Opener*	*Responder*	*Opener*	*Responder*
2 NT	No Bid	2 ♣	2 ◇	2 ♣	2 ◇
		2 NT	3 ♠	3 NT	4 ♠
		4 ♠	No Bid	No Bid	

There is no weakness take-out over partner's opening 2 NT. But see the Flint Transfer Bid.	Just enough now for a game in Spades. No certainty, but worth an effort.	Responder's 4 S is no stronger than a pass. Add a high card and the bid would be 5 S.

TWO BIDS

TABLE VII

Opener	High Card Points	Responder	Opener's Rebid
2 NT	0–3	Pass.	
21–22	4–9	3 NT or 3 of a 5 or 6-card suit.	Pass unconditionally. Raise with a fit or bid 3 NT. With a fit, a maximum and good controls make the cheapest cue bid (e.g. 3 S over 3 H, as a slam try).
Same pattern as 1 NT	11	4 NT or 5 of a 6-card suit.	Bid slam with 22.
	12	6 NT or 6 of a long suit.	Pass always—or nearly.
2 C followed by 2 NT	0–2	Pass (after 2 D over 2C).	
23–24	3–8	3 NT or a suit as above.	Pass or raise suit.
	9	4 NT or a suit as above.	Bid slam with maximum.
	10	6 NT or a suit as above.	Pass.
2 C followed by 3 NT	6	4 NT or 5 of a suit.	Bid the slam on 27.
25 or more	7	5 NT, 5 or 6 in a suit.	Bid slam on 26.
	8	6 NT or 6 in a suit.	Pass.

It is an advantage that the opening lead should run up to the big hand. Therefore, even when Responder has a long suit, the best contract is often in No Trumps.

TWO BIDS

Intermediate Two Bids

Opener

♠ A K Q J
♡ A 10 8 7 6 3
◇ A
♣ 3 2

Responder

	A			B			C	
♠	5 4 3		♠	10 8 7		♠	9 7	
♡	K Q 5 4		♡	J 5 4 2		♡	K Q 5	
◇	Q 7 6 3 2		◇	Q 10 6 3		◇	K 8 4 2	
♣	4		♣	Q 9		♣	A 10 8 5	

Opener	Responder	Opener	Responder	Opener	Responder
2 ♡	4 ♡	2 ♡	3 ♡	2 ♡	3 ♡
4 ♠	5 ♣	4 ♡	—	4 ♡	5 ♣
6 ♡				5 ◇	6 ♡
				7 ♡	

	D			E			F	
♠	9 7 3		♠	10 4 2		♠	10 6	
♡	9 2		♡	K 5		♡	4 2	
◇	Q J 7 6 2		◇	K Q 10 8 3		◇	7 6	
♣	J 6 4		♣	Q 7 4		♣	K Q J 10 9 7 4	

	D		E		F
Opener	Responder	Opener	Responder	Opener	Responder
2 ♡	2 NT	2 ♡	3 ◇	2 ♡	2 NT
3 ♡	No Bid	3 ♠	4 ♡	3 ♡	5 ♣
				6 ♣	

The first response is conventional and the bidding stops at 3 H.

The opening must be based on a good 5-card or on a 6-card suit. The Spades may be short.

Opener can see twelve tricks even though Responder lacks a trick and a half.

71

TWO BIDS

TABLE VIII

BIG DISTRIBUTIONAL HANDS—2 S: 2 H: 2 D

Opener	Responder	Opener's Rebid
Qualifications:	2 NT denies 1½ tricks.	With a two suiter, Opener should show his second suit, even when it is shorter than the first (7–5 and sometimes 6–4) on the second round.
Eight playing tricks	A Single Raise promises little except a minor fit.	
A 6-card suit or two good 5-card suits	With an Ace and a King show any worthwhile suit.	
	3 NT shows a balanced hand with 10–11 scattered points.	After showing a big hand Opener leaves the initiative for slamming to Responder.
Top cards in at least two suits	With good trump support, but no Ace, Jump Raise partner's suit. With solid suit, a Jump Response—e.g. 3 S over 2 H.	
2 C followed by 2 S: 2 H: 2 D: 3 C Unconditionally forcing to game	2 D denies 1½ tricks. With 1½ tricks show any worthwhile suit. On a balanced hand 2 NT with 8–9 points; 3 NT with 10–11 points.	Opener, having shown his suit over the negative response of 2 D, should rebid it, if it is long, because a 2 C opening, unlike an intermediate Two bid, does not guarantee a long (5-or 6-card) suit.

TWO BIDS

Caution at Rubber Bridge

At rubber bridge, with less than a trick and a half, it is wise to give a negative response—2 NT opposite an Intermediate Two bid and 2 D opposite 2 C.

Under the Acol system and also under CAB, the Intermediate Two bid is forcing for one round. On the second round Responder can pass on a worthless hand unless Opener jumps in a new suit.

Responses to Two Bids

Rigid rules once governed responses to Two Bids, but these have been progressively relaxed, and the trend continues.

Broadly speaking, an Ace and a King or two King-Queens, constitute a positive response, but by arrangement with partner these values may be shaded. They often are at the top of the bridge pyramid.

A Double Raise

With good trump support, but no Ace or void in the hand, Responder jump raises Opener's suit—e.g. 4 S over 2 S. This bid does not rule out a singleton and may be construed as a mild slam try. Note Responder's cue bid in Clubs on A (page 71). Opener knows that it is the *second round* control. With an Ace or void Responder would not have given a double raise.

The pattern of an unbalanced hand is often reproduced round the table and the best looking holdings are apt to be wrecked by adverse distribution. Hence the emphasis on a fit, for the vital question must always be: Where will the hand be played?

A Solid Suit

A solid suit of one's own is almost as good as a fit for partner's and there is a special way of announcing it—a jump. Opener calls 2 D and Responder bids 3 H with ♡ A K Q J 3 2 or 3 S with ♠ A K Q 9 7 6 2. The rest of the hand does not matter.

With ♠ K Q J 10 7 6 5 Responder *first* makes the denial bid of 2 NT, *then* jumps to 4 S. Opener will read this as saying: I lack a trick and a half, but my Spades are near solid. Holding ♠ A x he will reckon on six tricks opposite.

Once a trump suit has been established slam prospects can be investigated. The initiative, be it noted, should nearly always be taken by Responder, who knows more about Opener's strength than Opener knows about his.

Unlimited Hands

Unlimited hands are opened 2 C. As we saw above, an Ace and a King are required for the minimum positive response. But there is one exception. Balanced hands with 8–9 points qualify for a response of 2 NT if the honours are well distributed. With 10–11 points the bid is 3 NT but with more—especially if the hand contains two Aces—Responder should find some other bid.

With

	(1)	(2)	(3)
♠	K J 9	A K J 9	10 3
♡	Q 6 4	7 4 3 2	7 6 4
◇	Q 3 2	8 6 2	A K 9 7 4
♣	J 4 3 2	4 3	8 3 2

Responder bids 2 NT over 2 C on (1) but 2 S on (2) showing partner where his high cards are. On (3) the bid is 3 D since 2 D would be a denial.

If Opener's 2 C is the Acol super NT type, he still rebids 2 NT over 2 S or 2 H as he would do over the negative 2 D.

CAB

A feature of CAB, a 2 C system with a following among well-known players, is the Ace response to 2 C. Responder bids his Ace suit, even if it is a singleton, suppressing his longest suit until the next round. With two Aces the Cab response is 3 NT.

Since Aces are shown on the first round, a Blackwood 4 NT bid asks for Kings and 5 NT is an inquiry for Queens.

9

PRE-EMPTIVE BIDS

This chapter forges the natural link between attacking and defensive bidding, for a pre-emptive bid has the characteristics of both. It is constructive, since it initiates the auction. Yet its purpose is not to pave the way to the best contract, but to prevent opponents from reaching theirs, and in that sense, it is purely destructive—a piece of calculated sabotage.

An Advance Sacrifice

The player who opens 3 D or 3 H does not expect to make nine tricks. He expects to go down in a good cause. Fundamentally, a pre-emptive bid is an advance sacrifice—an offer to pay for erecting a barrage which will impede the exchange of information between opponents.

According to accepted standards, a fair price is three down non-vulnerable and two down vulnerable. That is the theory. In practice some of the best players take bigger chances, especially when opening Three of a major.

Qualifications for Three Bids

A Three bid is made normally on a hand with a 7-card suit and less than two defensive tricks—often with no defensive trick at all. The point count does not come into it, but it could be as low as 3 and is rarely higher than 9, ranging from:

♠ Q J 10 9 6 5 2 ♥ 2 ♦ 10 8 7 2 ♣ 2

to

♠ K Q J 5 4 3 2 ♥ 2 ♦ Q J 6 ♣ 3 2

PRE-EMPTIVE BIDS

Raising a Three Bid

Partner should not raise a Three bid in a major to Four, expecting to make it, unless he can contribute about four playing tricks.

Responder is often tempted to try the cheaper contract of 3 NT. This he can only do with a good fit for partner's suit, something like A x x or K x x, but never with a doubleton. Paradoxically, without a 3-card fit, he should raise Opener's suit—if his general holding warrants it. In No Trumps it is a question of entries. Opener is unlikely to have high cards outside his long suit, and if Responder has only a doubleton in it and becomes declarer at No Trumps, he may find that he has no access to dummy.

Raising on Bad Hands

Here is another paradox. With good distributional support, Responder should raise partner's suit on a *very bad* hand. When he has less than two defensive tricks it must be apparent to him that opponents have a certain game and perhaps a slam. Raising the pre-emptive barrage will be the best way to impede them or to steer them, maybe, into the wrong contract.

Opening Four in a Minor

In a minor a Three bid is not so effective a shut out as in a major and does not, therefore, justify quite the same risks.

An opening Four bid rules out 3 NT, the cheapest game bid of all, and is made rarely until partner has passed. Third in hand, however, at favourable vulnerability, this would be an opening 4 D:

♠ 2   ♡ 3 2   ◇ K Q 10 8 7 6 4 3   ♣ 3 2

Vulnerability

At unfavourable vulnerability, only the cheapest sacrifice

(one down) can be worth while and the requirements for pre-emptive bids must be tightened up accordingly.

Fourth Man Speaks

Fourth in hand, after three passes, there can be no question of shutting out opponents, for the hand can be thrown in. A Three bid in that situation suggests a long, solid suit and invites partner, if he has stoppers elsewhere, to call 3 NT.

Hand (1) below is a typical Three bid in any of the first three positions at the table:

(1)	♠ K J 10 8 7 6 5	(2)	♠ K Q J 9 8 7 2
	♡ 2		♡ 2
	♢ Q J 8		♢ A 7 4
	♣ 3 2		♣ 3 2

but (2) is too good. At equal or favourable vulnerability it is worth 4 S, which may shut out Hearts. At unfavourable vulnerability the best bid is 1 S.

Opening Four in a Major

There is a much wider margin between minimum and maximum for an opening Four bid in a major. The hand could be as good as (1) on page 68, which would qualify for a Two bid if all the tricks were not in the same suit. Or it could be no better than:

> ♠ K Q J 8 7 6 5
> ♡ 3
> ♢ K J 10 6
> ♣ 3

which is only slightly better than a Three bid.

Responder must bear this in mind when he feels that a slam may be in the offing. Without two controls, at least, he is rarely in a position to encourage Opener.

Examples of Responses

Responder holds:

(1) ♠ K 2
     ♡ A 3 2
     ◇ Q 10 3 2
     ♣ A K J 2

3 NT over 3 H
a reasonable speculation
which will succeed most of
the time.

4 NT over 4 H (Blackwood)
If partner has an Ace, 6 H
is a legitimate gamble,
though no certainty.

(2) ♠ A 2
     ♡ K 2
     ◇ 4 3 2
     ♣ A K 5 4 3 2

4 H over 3 H

6 H over 4 H
After making certain, through
Blackwood, that Opener has an
Ace.

(3) ♠ A K J 10 9 6
     ♡ —
     ◇ A J 7 6
     ♣ K 3 2

No Bid over 3 H or 4 H

Never rescue a pre-emptive
bid. In bridge, the word
'never' means 'hardly ever'.

(4) ♠ A K Q 10 9 6
     ♡ Q 8 2
     ◇ —
     ♣ A 4 3 2

5 NT over 4 H

(The Grand Slam Force)
If partner has ♡ A K you want
to be in Seven. Over 3 H, even
6 H cannot be guaranteed,
though it should be bid.

(5) ♠ K 7 6 4 2
     ♡ 4 3 2
     ◇ J 7 6 3
     ♣ 2

4 S over 3 S
Even 5 S is justified for
opponents must be in the
slam zone—even the grand
slam zone.

(6) ♠ —
     ♡ A J 3
     ◇ K 3 2
     ♣ A K Q J 7 4 2

3 NT over 3 S
Partner, having described his
hand, is not expected to bid
again.

78

PRE-EMPTIVE BIDS

Counter action against pre-emptive bids by the other side will be discussed later, for it belongs essentially to the mechanics of defensive bidding.

10

DEFENSIVE BIDDING

An intervening call—or butt-in, as it is often known—serves more than one purpose. A hand may 'belong' to either side and the primary object of an overcall is to enter a tentative claim for the defenders. When they have the balance of power, the claim can be pressed successfully, the roles are then reversed and the defenders become the attackers.

More often, the cards are fairly evenly divided or else the hand belongs to Opener and his partner. Then the bidding becomes competitive and each side strives to push the other out of its depth or to find a cheap sacrifice.

Responder relies on the values disclosed by the opening. A defender, too, must be able to depend on his partner's intervening bid when he has to decide how far it is safe to push the other side and when they have been pushed far enough. It follows that an overcall must have defensive strength, as well as playing tricks. The latter without the former is not enough by itself, for it would not tell partner when opponents had overstepped the mark.

Still another object of an intervening bid is to indicate an effective opening lead in defence—one which partner would be unlikely to find by himself.

Playing Tricks

In defensive bidding the number of playing tricks in a hand is more important than its point count. That is why only in exceptional circumstances is an overcall made on a 4-card suit. Usually it is a suit of at least five cards headed by the Ace or King or by two lesser honours.

Middle Cards

When counting playing tricks, the middle cards—often

shown as xs in diagrams—must be treated with special respect.

What is the value of this combination: Q J x x x x? The answer depends on the xs. If they represent the 10 9 8 7, four tricks will be made. If they are the 5 4 3 2 the value must be written down to a fraction over three. Whenever in doubt about whether or not to butt-in, be guided by the texture of the suit.

Choice of Weapons

Though experts do not all adhere to the same standards, Table IX shows what are generally accepted as the normal requirements. A wide range of weapons is available in defence. The simple overcall is the least powerful and the most common, though it gains strength with vulnerability and more still when made at the level of Two.

The Jump Overcall

Much stronger is the Jump Overcall—e.g. 2 H over an opponent's 1 C. With its promise of about seven playing tricks and a good suit, it invites partner to bid game on the slenderest values, either in a major or—if the jump bid was in a minor—in No Trumps (see (6) p. 84).

Weak, pre-emptive jump overcalls are much in vogue across the Atlantic. In Britain this variation was tried out in the immediate post-war period (by the Baron team), but is rarely used today.

1 NT Overcall

With a double guard in the suit bid by Right Hand Opponent and a balanced hand in the 16–18 group, the correct defensive bid is 1 NT. And with 20–22 the classical overcall is 2 NT.

These bids, and more especially the latter, may, however, be turned also to other purposes. The Baron method was to use the 1 NT overcall as a weak informatory double and there exist today several variations on this theme.

The Unusual No Trump

Growing in popularity is the American version, associated

with the Roth-Stone system, of treating a 1 NT overcall, in certain circumstances, as a request to partner for his longest minor. The convention comes into operation when it is clear that the bidder cannot have a *natural* No Trump overcall— i.e. a balanced 16–18 hand.

This would be a typical example: Partner passes. After two more passes his RHO bids 1 S and partner now calls 1 NT. What are the inferences? With anything like a 16 point hand partner would not have passed in the first place. And with a distributional three-suiter, he would double on the second round. Why does he not double? Presumably because he is weak in Hearts. It follows by a process of elimination, that his strength is in the minors.

2 NT Overcall

The Unusual No Trump is used often at the Two level. After an enemy sequence of 1 S—2 S an overcall of 2 NT could mean little else than a show of interest in the minors. On a strong hand, with Hearts as well as the minors, the caller would double.

A Question of Frequency

As so much else in bidding, it comes down to a question of frequency. Hands in the 20–22 range come up rarely after an opponent has opened the bidding. Occasions for contesting the auction with distributional Club-Diamond holdings arise more often. Hence the popularity of what has become known as the Unusual No Trump. Many tournament players today use a *jump* 2 NT overcall (e.g. 2 NT over an opponent's 1 H or 1 S) only in this sense.

The Informatory Double

This, the oldest bidding convention in Contract Bridge, is also the most flexible. Its purpose is to invite partner to buy the contract in *his* best suit. It follows that the defender who doubles must have support for the other three suits. Or else, if he has a weak spot, he must have a suit of his own which he can bid, over partner's, should the need arise.

Defensive Bids

TABLE IX

	Non-Vulnerable	Vulnerable
Simple Overcall (e.g. 1 S over 1 H)	a 5 or 6-card suit 4 playing tricks 1½ defensive tricks	a *fair* 5 or 6-card suit 4½ playing tricks 1½ defensive tricks
Overbid at the Two level	a *fair* 5 or 6-card suit 5½ playing tricks 2 defensive tricks	a *good* 5 or 6-card suit 6 playing tricks 2½ defensive tricks

Regardless of Vulnerability

Jump Overbid (e.g. 2S over 1 D)	a good 6 or 7-card suit 7–8 playing tricks 2½–3 defensive tricks
1 NT	A balanced hand of 16–18 points and a double guard in opponent's suit
Double	On a balanced hand, with support for the unbid major(s), the minimum is 15–16. This may be scaled down according to shape to as little as 11–12 on 4-4-4-1 or 5-4-4-0, especially at favourable vulnerability.
Cue Bid in Opponent's Suit	The strongest of all defensive bids, this shows both high cards and distribution and calls on partner to keep open the bidding till game is reached.

Game All. Your Right Hand opponent deals and bids 1 H. You hold:

	(1)		(2)		(3)
♠	J 9 5 4 2	♠	K 10 7 6	♠	4 2
♡	7 2	♡	4 2	♡	Q 10 2
◇	A Q 4	◇	A J 9	◇	A K 9 2
♣	K 9 3	♣	K Q J 9	♣	K Q J 2

83

DEFENSIVE BIDDING

(1) *No Bid.* The suit is too poor for a vulnerable overcall. Non-vulnerable it would be a borderline case for butting in with 1 S, though many players* would pass unhesitatingly regardless of vulnerability.

(2) *Double.* You want to know partner's suit and you can support whichever suit he bids.

(3) *No Bid.* A slightly better hand than the last, but with nothing in Spades a double would be unwise. The temptation to bid 2 C on a 4-card suit should be resisted, but even that would be preferable to a double.

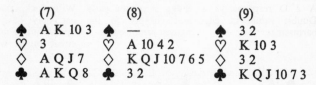

	(4)	(5)	(6)
♠	Q 4	Q	K 2
♡	A J 9	A Q J 3 2	4 2
◇	K Q J 7 6	A J 7	A K Q J 7 3
♣	K 8 7	K J 3 2	Q 10 3

(4) *1 NT.* About a minimum.

(5) *No Bid.* With so much in opponent's suit silence is the best form of speech.

(6) *3 D.* With a hope and a Heart stop partner will bid 3 NT, which is what you hope he will do.

	(7)	(8)	(9)
♠	A K 10 3	—	3 2
♡	3	A 10 4 2	K 10 3
◇	A Q J 7	K Q J 10 7 6 5	3 2
♣	A K Q 8	3 2	K Q J 10 7 3

(7) *2 H.* This, the strongest of all defensive bids, will ensure that partner keeps the bidding open till game. You will have space, meanwhile, to find your best fit.

(8) *4 D.* In pre-empting raise the level as high as you dare *at once.* You may shut out Spades or lure opponents into an unmakable contract in Hearts.

(9) *2 C.* A sub-minimum bid redeemed by the value of a Club lead in defence, especially against No Trumps.

* Including the author.

DEFENSIVE BIDDING

The Informatory Double

EXAMPLE

North deals and opens 1 H. East, sitting over him, holds:

	A	B	C

A
♠ J 10 8 4
♡ 3 2
◇ A K Q 8 6
♣ A 2

B
♠ A 5
♡ Q 10 9 8
◇ Q 5 4 3 2
♣ A K

C
♠ K 3 2
♡ A Q
◇ A 10 9 8 7
♣ A 9 7

A
Double
Every card is well-placed —for attack.

B
No Bid
So much stronger in defence than in attack.

C
1 NT
Partner will know what to do.

D
♠ A 9 8
♡ 9 6 2
◇ 4 2
♣ A K Q 8 2

E
♠ A K 10 8 3
♡ 2
◇ K 10 9 4
♣ Q J 3

F
♠ Q J 3
♡ 2
◇ A K 10 8 3
♣ K 10 9 4

D
2 Clubs
A 2 D response to a Double would be embarrassing.

E
1 Spade
Stake a claim early and cheaply to the highest ranking suit.

F
Double
With luck, partner may have a Spade suit. If not, either minor will do.

G
♠ A 2
♡ K J 10 4 2
◇ K J 5 4 2
♣ Q

H
♠ 3 2
♡ A K J 7 6 4
◇ A 6
♣ Q 4 2

I
♠ 10 2
♡ K 3
◇ A K Q J 7 6 4
♣ A 2

G
No Bid
Sit back, hoping that opponents will get into trouble. An overcall of 2 D is unlikely to prove constructive.

H
No Bid
See what happens, before committing yourself. *Don't* bid 1 NT.

I
3 NT
A very mild but obvious gamble. No reasonable alternative presents itself.

DEFENSIVE BIDDING

TABLE X

The Informatory Double Distribution	High Card Points	High Card Points	Second Defender's Response
5–4–4–0	11	0–8	Make the cheapest bid but always a major before a minor
4–4–4–1	11–12	9–10	With a 4-card major jump (e.g. 2 H over 1 D doubled)
5–4–3–1	13	11–12	Jump in a major or a minor. With a 6-card major bid game directly
5–4–2–2 5–3–3–2	14		
4–4–3–2	15	13	Cue bid in opponent's suit
4–3–3–3	16	—	With length in the suit bid by the other side, you may leave in the double for penalties.

DEFENSIVE BIDDING

To make an informatory double a player should have about 15–16 points, though much of this may be distributional. Implicit in the double is the promise of a fit for partner and the 3–2–1 scale of ruffing values—a conservative scale by common consent—is used liberally to swell the total of high card points. And since the Spade suit, being the highest in rank, is worth more than the others, a defender may shade his double a little if his Spades are good. Conversely, weakness in Spades must always be a deterrent.

If the opening bid is 1 S an informatory double should be stronger than if the opening were 1 C. Over the double of 1 C partner can call his suit, any suit, at the One level. Over 1 S he can show no suit under the level of Two.

Defence or Attack?

Though distribution is a key factor, a defender may still double, without shape, on 16 or better. But he should not try too hard. And if much of his strength lies in the suit bid by the other side, he usually does best to pass. Such hands are more suited for defence than for attack and the informatory double is, above all, an attacking weapon. Example (5) on page 84 points the moral. Compare also A and B on page 85. On A every card is where it should be and the 5—4—2—2 pattern is at

its dubious best, giving defenders the opportunity to seize the initiative. On B the honours and even the middle cards are largely wasted for purposes of attack, though combined with the distribution, they endow the hand with impressive values in defence.

On C an informatory double is purposeless for the interest lies, not in partner's suit, but in his strength, wherever it may be.

Responses to a Double

With nothing at all the second defender must still respond to his partner's informatory double. Therefore, with even a modest holding, he must do better than that. To show the difference between something and nothing, the second defender *jumps*—he bids one more than is necessary to overcall the opening bid (compare (a) and (b) below) on 9 points or better.

A Major before a Minor

Knowing that he can depend on a fit for a major, doubler's partner should show a 4-card major in preference to a 5-card minor. It is more likely to lead to a game contract and is therefore more constructive. And since the double is apt to be largely distributional, partner should avoid, if he can, responding in No Trumps.

Direct Jump to Game

With a 6-card major and 9 points or better, he jumps directly to game. There is not enough for a slam and no further information need be given or received on the way to game. It is best, therefore, to crowd the bidding for the other side, in case they can get together for a worthwhile sacrifice. (See (c) below.)

The Informatory Double: Responses by the Second Defender

Game All. Your Left Hand Opponent bids 1 D, partner doubles and your Right Hand Opponent passes. You hold:

(a)	(b)	(c)
♠ 5 4 3 2	♠ Q J 4 2	♠ K J 10 7 6 4
♡ J 7	♡ 8 7	♡ A J
◇ 8 3	◇ 9 3	◇ 4 3 2
♣ 10 8 5 3 2	♣ A J 10 9 6	♣ 7 5

(a) *1 S.* It is cheaper than 2 C and *any* 4-card suit is biddable in response to a double.

(b) *2 S.* So much better than you might be—e.g. (a).

(c) *4 S.* A direct quantitative bid, which should shut out opponents. There is no prospect of a slam and no question of stopping short of game.

(d)	(e)	(f)
♠ Q 4	♠ K 10 4 2	♠ K J 10 7 6 4
♡ J 10 3	♡ K 9 7 6	♡ A 6
◇ Q J 10 8 6 3	◇ K 2	◇ 2
♣ 4 2	♣ A 10 3	♣ A Q J 10

(d) *No Bid.* You should take four tricks in defence and can expect a penalty of 500 or so. In attack your hand is pretty useless.

(e) *2 D.* You want to announce game values and to induce partner to show *his* suit. The cue bid in opponents' suit will give you time to get together.

(f) *2 D.* Whatever partner bids, jump in Spades. This sequence will show him a big hand with slam aspirations and a good, long suit.

A Jump Not Forcing

Unlike all other jump bids by a partner who has not previously passed, a jump bid in response to a double is *not forcing*. The bid is invitational by implication, but it is limited and the doubler can pass.

Cue Bid in Opponent's Suit

If the second defender is good enough to envisage game opposite a minimum double he must do more than jump. He should *cue bid* the *opponent's* suit. In response to the double of, say, 1 Club, the bid is *2 Clubs* (see (e) and (f) above). Except by players in the master class this weapon is not used enough. It gives the partnership time to look for the best contract, especially when the second defender has four cards in both majors and wants his partner to pick the one in which he is longest. The cue bid of an opponent's suit at a low level does *not* always promise the first round control.

If the first defender makes the cue bid he shows a hand

which he expects to yield game virtually on its own (as in (7) page 84). If the bid is made by the second defender, in response to an informatory double, it shows only a game hand on the *combined holdings* ((e) page 89). Any hand worth an opening bid qualifies.

The Penalty Pass

There are times when the second defender can pass his partner's double. This he does not when he is weak or when he has no biddable suit, but when he holds sufficient strength in an opponent's suit to hold out the prospect of a penalty. At favourable vulnerability the responder to a double may leave it in on a good hand with high cards outside the trump suit. With the vulnerability reversed a penalty pass, as it is known, is made usually on a poor hand with five or six trumps, but no outside strength and no length in a major (see (d) on page 89).

When Opponents Call Two Suits

When opponents have bid two suits an informatory double asks partner to choose one of the other two. The emphasis on distribution may be greater than when one suit only has been bid and partner should not hesitate to call a 3-card suit, and even to jump on a 3-card suit, if his values are in the right places. Here is an illustration:

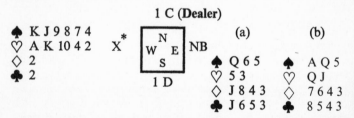

1 C **(Dealer)**

(a)   (b)

North deals and opens 1 C. East passes, South bids 1 D and West doubles. Assuming that North passes the double, East calls:

---

* X is the conventional sign for Double

1 S on (a) and *2 S* on (b)

He need not hesitate to jump on (b) for his four high cards are just where they are wanted. On the bidding, partner must have length in both majors and it is not essential for East to have four cards in either.

Counter to Pre-emptive Bids

As a counter to pre-emptive bids by opponents more than one method is in current use. In principle the situation is much the same as in the case of an ordinary informatory double and in the United States no radical distinction is made, whether the opening is at the level of One or Three.

For this there is a price to pay. The player sitting over the opening bidder cannot make a penalty double, and as pre-emptive bids are often foolhardy and sometimes reckless, this is an undoubted liability.

Doubling for Penalties

The practice in Britain is to treat the double of an opening Three bid as primarily for penalties. To invite a bid from part-ner we use one of three conventional devices. We call: (1) 3 NT or (2) 4 C or (3) the next higher ranking suit at the lowest level.

Whichever convention we use, partner may have to respond at the level of Four. Consequently we must be good and some-times we should be ready to run risks, which is only fair since by pre-empting the other side runs risks, too.

3 NT for a Take-Out

Over an opening 3 S a take-out bid of 3 NT (or 4 C) is made on something like:

♠ 2
♡ A K 9 7
◇ K Q 10 4 2
♣ A J 9

in short, a strong informatory double.

DEFENSIVE BIDDING

Lowest Minor

If you use the 4 C convention the equivalent of an informatory double over 3 C is 3 D. That is why the convention is often known as 'the lowest minor'.

Herbert or Fishbein

The third convention—less popular than the other two—enjoins a call in the next higher ranking suit. Over 3 D it is 3 H, over 3 H it is 3 S and over 3 S it is 4 C—not 3 NT, which is used naturally. This convention is known variously as Herbert or Fishbein.

In the 3 NT school, which expresses the majority view among public and masters alike, a trend is developing to treat the double of an opening bid in a minor as two-way. On a balanced hand partner leaves in the double for penalties. With length in a suit he bids it, and if he is worth it, he jumps. This approach to opponents' Three bids is eminently flexible and economizes space and time in bidding.

4 NT for a Take-Out

Over an opening bid at the Four level 4 NT always demands a take out and a double is always for penalties—that is, nearly always. Allowance must be made for situations such as this:

Your left hand opponent calls 4 S, partner doubles, next man passes and you hold:

♠ 7 6 5 4
♡ K Q 10 6 5 3
◇ 4
♣ K 7

Since Opener must have seven or eight Spades, partner has two or one or none. Yet he doubled. Obviously he has high cards in the other suits, but dare not commit himself to the Five level by calling 4 NT. For one thing he must surely be weak in Hearts.

It follows that, although the double is for penalties, you should have no hesitation in calling 5 H, especially at unfavourable vulnerability. Even 6 H must be given serious consideration.

Partnership Understanding

As we have just seen, there are several ways of countering pre-emptive bids, but partnership understanding is by far the most important consideration involved. In this, as in so many other fields, it is best at rubber bridge to conform to partner's habits and inclinations. The superiority of one method over another is relatively slight. The importance of following the same method, even if it is inferior, is decisive.

11

FREE BIDS

By intervening defenders restrict freedom of movement for the other side. New conditions come into being and values, which hold good in an undisputed auction, must be modified.

Responder need strive no longer to keep the bidding open, for defenders have done that already. If Responder bids over a butt-in it is, therefore, a *free bid* and may be worth a little more than if the opponent on his right had passed. But how much more? Many players want about 2 points extra, but it would be wrong to accept this or any other rigid standard, for a free bid does not promise the same values in different situations.

Free Bid after a Double

A special case, in a class by itself, arises after an informatory double. Let us take up the thread from the last chapter. Opener calls 1 Diamond and his Left Hand Opponent doubles.

Any bid by Third Man now shows weakness, maybe even dire distress. His hand may be:

♠ 7 6   ♡ J 10 8 6 3 2   ◇ 7   ♣ 10 8 7 2

in which case he may well fear that Second Defender will leave in the double for a penalty, as in (d), page 89. As a rescue operation Third Man will bid 1 Heart, while there is still time. It is true that he might insert a bid on a better hand, say: ♠ 7 6 ♡ K J 9 8 4 ◇ 8 5 ♣ K 10 3 2, fearing that if he passes, it will be too late to come in on the next round, over 2 Spades or 3 Clubs, perhaps. For the same reason, he might bid 1 NT, over the double, on a balanced hand worth 7 or 8 points. It would be a case of now or never. But broadly speaking, any bid by Responder after a double shows weakness.

94

FREE BIDS

Distributional Raises

With little high card strength, but distributional support for Opener's suit, Responder should raise it at once over the double, as high as he dare, overbidding his hand by about a trick or 2–3 points, to crowd the auction for opponents (see *A*, below). At favourable vulnerability, still bigger risks may be taken.

The Re-Double

On a fair hand, but *without* length in Opener's suit, Responder's best course, usually, is to re-double. This tells partner that the balance of strength is against opponents and that defence may be more profitable than attack (see *B*, below).

A re-double calls for the same type of hand as an informatory double—*shortage in partner's suit* and some high cards outside. About 9–10 points suffice.

Action by Third Man after an Informatory Double

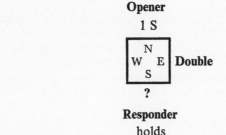

Opener

1 S

W E **Double**

?

Responder
holds

A	*B*	*C*
♠ J 7 6 4	♠ 2	♠ J 5 4 2
♡ 3	♡ K 10 7 6	♡ A
♢ K J 9 4 2	♢ Q 9 7 3	♢ K J 10
♣ Q 7 3	♣ A 9 6 2	♣ A J 7 3 2

A. 3 S. Without East's double, 2 S would be enough. Now, with so little defence, especially against Hearts, every effort should be made to shut out West, the second defender.

B. Re-double. You want to defend on this hand, for you expect to double profitably any bid made by the other side at the Two level. And if 1 S re-doubled is left in, which is unlikely, you need have no undue fears. With your high cards partner should be able to make seven tricks. Alternatively, if his suit is short and poor, he can take himself out. After all, he knows what your re-double means.

C. Re-double. An unusual type of re-double and very different from *B*. Should opponents call 2 D, jump to 4 S. Over 2 H, bid 3 H. There should be distinct slam possibilities here and bold action is imperative.

D

♠ 2
♡ 10 9 8 6 5 4
◇ 4 3 2
♣ 4 3 2

D. 2 H. This is a routine take out. Responder fears a crash in 1 S doubled, which the second defender may leave in. The rescue bid promises no strength whatever—not a single point.

Opener, however, does not expect such abject weakness— just as he does not expect so formidable a hand as *C* from partner's re-double.

A jump in Opener's suit, after a re-double on the previous round, suggests that Responder has no fear of a sacrifice by Opponents, and also that he sees the possibility of a slam if Opener has something to spare. This situation, however, is comparatively rare. A re-double usually indicates a shortage in Opener's suit and a desire to double opponents. In short, *B* not *C* is the common type.

With a hand unsuitable for defence, Opener will try to show a second suit, for he has been warned by the re-double that partner is short in his first. Otherwise he will look for a penalty and will either double any bid made by the other side or pass it round to Responder, who should be able to take some action.

FREE BIDS

Free Bid over Re-double

A re-double or any other bid by Third Man allows the second defender—doubler's partner—to pass if he has nothing to say. If he speaks, he should have something though it need not be much. His partner has asked him to show a suit and he should try to co-operate. With a major, which can be shown at the One level, almost any holding will justify a bid.

At one time it was the practice to ignore the re-double and to pass only if there was a desire to defend the re-doubled contract of One. This variation is rarely used in modern bidding. A pass over a re-double today would indicate a very poor hand and the inability to make a cheap, constructive bid.

Free Bids after an Overcall

Action by Opener's partner after an overcall by a defender falls under two headings. The first covers bids which are not affected by the butt-in. The second lists those which must be modified or even abandoned altogether.

Pride of place in the first group goes to limit bids—raises in partner's suit and in No Trumps. Admittedly, a jump to 2 or 3 No Trumps indicates a sound guard in opponents' suit, but no additional all-round strength is required (see *E*, page 98).

Raises in Opener's suit remain much the same (see *G*, page 98) despite the butt-in, though if the decision is close Responder may take a conservative view calling, say, 2 Hearts instead of stretching to bid 3 Hearts.

Action by Third Man after an Overcall

Opener

1 D

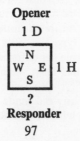

?

Responder

Responder holds:

E	F	G
♠ Q 9 6	♠ K J 9 4	♠ Q 9 6
♡ A J 4	♡ 7 3	♡ 9 4
◊ 10 4	◊ 10 4 2	◊ K 7 6 4
♣ K J 7 6 5	♣ A 8 4 2	♣ Q J 3 2

E. 2 NT. A natural bid, unaffected by the butt-in. Partner can pass, of course, if he opened on a minimum. Or he can sign off in 3 D, if he has a long suit, but a weak hand unsuitable for No Trumps.

F. 1 S. That would have been the bid if East had passed, and there is no reason why the butt-in should make any difference. Though it is a free bid, it cannot complicate Opener's rebid.

G. 2 D. The intervening bid should not deter Responder from showing modest support for partner's suit. Without the butt-in he might have called 1 NT. Since he has no stop in Hearts, Responder must fall back on 2 D, but he must say something constructive.

H
♠ A Q J 2
♡ 6
◊ K 9 4
♣ A Q 10 3 2

H. 3 C. Responder's hand has improved. The butt-in suggests that the missing honours in the black suits are more likely to be under than over the Aces.

An intervening bid should not deter a player from making a forcing take-out.

Free Bid in New Suit

If he can show a suit at the One level Responder should still do so after an intervening bid, unless he has an absolute minimum. If his suit is biddable, 7–8 points should be enough most of the time (see *F*, page 98). Since Opener must have been prepared for any response at the level of One, his rebid will not be complicated. And that is the crux of the matter and the reason for the different treatment of hands in the second group.

When Free Bids Must be Stronger

When making a free bid Responder must have something to spare, *if he raises the level* of partner's rebid (see *I*, but also *J*, page 100).

Opener calls 1 Club, ready to rebid 1 Spade or 1 No Trump on the next round. But suppose that a defender butts-in with 1 Heart and partner calls 2 Diamonds. Opener is now compelled to call *2 Spades* or *2 No Trumps*.

Or let us say that the opening is 1 Spade and the intended rebid is 2 Spades. If a defender intervenes with 2 Diamonds and Responder calls 3 Clubs, Opener will have to call 3 Spades. For, despite the butt-in, he is still obliged to find a second bid after a response in a new suit.

Free Bid after 1 No Trump

Finally, after an intervening bid (except a double), there can be no such thing as a weakness take-out of 1 No Trump. If Responder calls a suit, it must be constructive. He is not looking for game, but he is ready to compete in the auction. With a poor 5-or 6-card suit, and nothing outside, he passes, though that is the type of hand on which, without the butt-in, he would call his suit.

Low Level Doubles

One of the most useful words in Responder's vocabulary is: *Double*. It does not require great strength. It is informative. And it cannot complicate Opener's rebid (see *K*, page 100).

FREE BIDS

Action by Third Man after an Overcall at the Two level

1 S

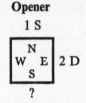

?

Responder

holds

	I	*J*	*K*

I. *2 S.* You were going to bid 2 C, but you are not good enough to bid at the Three level, so show your slender fit for partner's suit. The butt-in compels you to alter your bid—but not to forgo it.

J. *3 S.* You are worth a double raise, as you were before. The intervening bid does not affect the measure of your support for partner's suit.

K. *Double.* You should make about four tricks in defence— more than enough. If Opponents rescue themselves into Hearts, and partner doubles, you will be perfectly happy. Defence suits you better than attack and that is the message your double will convey to partner.

L

♠ 9 4
♡ J 8 7 3
◇ A K 10
♣ K 9 6 4

L. *? ? ?* The answer depends on vulnerability. If your side

100

alone is vulnerable, call 2 NT. If it is the other way, double.

At equal vulnerability the decision must be very close.

It often happens that Responder has enough to say something after a butt-in, but the wrong cards somehow for any given bid—too short in Opener's suit to raise it, no suit of his own and the wrong shape for No Trumps. At times he must pass regretfully. At others—with four useful cards in the enemy suit and a count of 9 or more—a double is the answer. It is *tentative* and Opener can take it out if it does not suit him. On a balanced hand, however, he may be glad of an opportunity to switch from attack to defence and to look for a penalty when a score below the line is uncertain. And that is the primary purpose of what is sometimes known as a 'snap double'—to warn partner of a misfit and to suggest defence in lieu of attack.

Opener must not expect the double to be based on great length or strength in the suit bid by the other side. On a distributional hand, with less defensive strength than partner is entitled to rely upon, Opener need not hesitate to remove the double.

A Snap Double must be Prepared

Responder, for his part, must resist the temptation to double a butt-in unless his hand is *generally suited* for defence.

Opener bids 1 S and the next player calls 2 D.

Responder holds:

	(1)		(2)
♠	7		Q 7 6
♡	5 3		3
♢	K J 9 8 7 6		K J 9 8 7 6
♣	J 4 3 2		J 3 2

Should he double?

Of course, he can expect to defeat 2 D by two, three, and perhaps by four tricks. But it is highly improbable that the hand will be played in Diamonds. One or other of the opponents will surely call 2 H, and Opener—who has been invited to switch from attack to defence—will very likely double.

What will Responder do then?

On (1) he will have no way out, though he will have every reason to expect 2 H doubled to be made, probably with an overtrick. In short, a double of 2 D, on (1) is unprepared for the next move. It is also misleading, for Opener will expect some general values in defence, and they are not there.

On (2) Responder can retreat to 2 S. But it is still a bad double. When a hand justifies one bid only, it is best, whenever possible, to show support for partner's suit. A simple raise in Spades has the added advantage of making it more difficult for the second defender to bid Hearts—a move which Responder naturally wishes to discourage.

Opener's Rebids after Free Bid by Responder

Opener

1 S

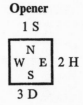

2 H

3 D

Opener holds:

M	N	O
♠ A J 7 6 2	♠ A J 7 6 2	♠ A J 7 6 2
♡ 4 3	♡ A J 9	♡ 6
◇ K 7 6	◇ J 3	◇ K J 3
♣ A J 9	♣ Q 10 3	♣ A K 10 3

M. 3 S. This shows five Spades, but nothing over a minimum. The level was raised by Responder.

N. 3 NT. With a double guard in Hearts, 3 NT becomes the natural rebid and shows no particular strength.

O. 4 C. A new suit at the Four level must be strong. Next time, Opener will raise Diamonds, revealing his shape as well.

He must feel hopeful, after hearing Responder's 3 D, that the partnership is on the way to a slam.

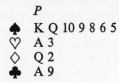

P. *4 S*. The alternative is 3 H, a cue-bid in the enemy suit.

Compare this hand with M above. Opener must make a distinction between two hands one of which is so much better than the other. The jump to 4 S shows that without the butt-in, over 2 D from partner, he would have bid 3 S at least.

Opener's Reactions to a Snap Double

Opener

1 S

Double

Opener holds:

	Q	*R*	*S*
♠	K J 10 7 6	10 9 8 7 6 5	A K Q J 7 6
♡	Q J 9 4	A K 2	J 9 4
◇	A 2	2	2
♣	J 7	A K 2	A 10 3

Q. *2 H*. With only one certain trick in defence it would be unwise to stand the double. If Responder is short in Spades, as his double suggests, he may well have a good fit in Hearts.

R. *No Bid*. A very suitable hand to stand the double. Partner can hardly expect more than four defensive tricks and there is a good chance, that with ready entries to Opener's hand, he will ruff one or more Spades.

S. 3 NT. Responder should be able to contribute two playing tricks, which will be enough for game.

T

♠ J 7 6 5 4 2
♡ K Q 8
◇ 2
♣ K Q 2

T. No Bid. This is not a very suitable hand to defend 2 D, but there is no alternative. Since partner may well have a singleton Spade, it is less risky to stand the double than to rescue into 2 S. It is a question of choosing the lesser of two evils.

Opener's Co-operation in Low Level Doubles

Opener (dealer)

1 S

2 H

2 D

Responder

X

North, the dealer, opens 1 S. East calls 2 D, which South doubles. West takes it out into 2 H. What action should North take?

North, Opener, holds:

U	*V*	*W*
♠ A 7 6 5 4	♠ K J 10 5 2	♠ K Q J 10 8 6
♡ A 10 8	♡ A K 2	♡ K 10 4
◇ 2	◇ 3 2	◇ 3
♣ A 8 6 3	♣ Q 7 6	♣ K Q 4

U. Double. Opener's hand is very suitable for defence against

2 H. He will lead the ♠ Ace and follow with another ♠. If partner does not ruff, he will surely do so next time. And Opener will still have an Ace to gain the lead for playing another Spade. Even if partner is over-ruffed, Opener's H 10 may be promoted.

V. No Bid. Opponents will probably go down, but it is too close to double, despite the tops in Hearts.

W. 3 S. Partner does not like Spades, but it does not matter. He will realize that Opener's suit is pretty solid, but that he needs tops to make game.

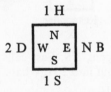

X

♠ A K Q J 6
♡ K 2
♢ 7 4
♣ K Q 7 3

X. 3 NT. The alternative is 3 C, but Opener wants to be declarer, so that the lead—if it is a Heart—should run up to his hand.

Since the double of 2 D is constructive, the side should have enough for game.

Opener's Free Rebids

1 H

2 D | N W E | N B
S

1 S

North deals and opens 1 H. His L.H.O. passes, partner responds 1 S and West, the second defender, comes in with 2 D. North holds:

(1)	(2)	(3)
♠ 9 7 4 2	♠ 7 4	♠ 4 2
♡ A 7 6 5 3	♡ A 7 6 5 3	♡ A K Q 10 8 6
♢ K 7	♢ K 9 7	♢ K 9 7
♣ A Q	♣ A Q 2	♣ 8 7

What should North bid?

(1) *2 S.* It is a minimum hand in high card points, but it is worth something extra in support of partner. If North passes now, he may never have the opportunity to show his liking for Spades.

(2) *No Bid.* Without West's overcall, North's rebid would be 2 H. But he has nothing to spare and he is not too proud of his suit. The intervening bid gives him the chance to describe his hand *by passing.*

(3) *2 H.* With a good suit and six, if not seven, playing tricks there need be no hesitation in making a free rebid.

And on . . .

	(4)	(5)	(6)
♠	7	A 8	Q 6
♡	A K 5 3 2	10 7 6 4 2	A Q 9 4
◇	J 9 4 2	7 3	K 10 3
♣	A 6 3	A K Q 7	A Q 7 3

North should . . . ?

(4) *Double.* This shows no extra strength but suggests that defence may be more profitable than attack. By implication the double proclaims a shortage in partner's suit.

(5) *No Bid.* Without the overcall the rebid would have been 2 C, but the hand is not good enough for a bid at the Three level and the Hearts are too poor to justify a free rebid of 2 H.

(6) *2 NT or Double*—according to vulnerability. North would have rebid 2 NT without the intervening bid and he can still do so. In fact, the overcall has improved his holding, suggesting that the missing Kings will be under the A Qs. At favourable vulnerability, however, a penalty may be more remunerative than game. If opponents are not vulnerable, 2 NT is the better bid, though only just.

Double of 1 No Trump

In a special category is the double of 1 NT. It is in no sense informatory. It is not even tentative. Primarily, it is a business double, though partner can take it out on a worthless hand with a 5 or 6-card suit—the sort of holding on which it would be proper to make a weakness take-out of partner's opening 1 NT.

To double an opening bid of 1 No Trump calls, therefore, for a powerful hand. To double an *intervening* 1 NT demands no more than 8 or 9 points, for if Opener has 13 and Responder 8, that is enough to establish a balance of power. And why should one side make more than half the tricks when the other has more than half the strength of the pack?

Opener—After a Free Bid

We have seen how Responder defers to Opener, how he never makes a free bid without taking into account the embarrassment which it might cause his partner. Opener allows for it. Whenever he can, he makes his natural rebid. But if the level has been raised against him, he is not unduly worried. He trusts Responder, who must have known what he was doing, and could presumably afford the higher level to which he pushed the auction.

Opener's Free Rebids

At the same time, Opener's promise to rebid, over a response in a different suit by partner, ceases to be binding if the *second* defender intervenes. Since opponents are keeping the bidding open and Responder will have another chance to speak, Opener may pass if it suits him to do so. A free rebid *may*, therefore, show something over a minimum. But it does not necessarily do so.

For Opener, as for Responder, the same reasoning applies. The fact that a bid is no longer obligatory makes a difference. But it is more important to be constructive than to be cautious and support for partner should be shown even on a minimum holding. So should a good, rebiddable suit.

There are times when it is convenient to limit the hand by

passing, but by and large, opponents should not be allowed to wrest the initiative too easily.

The S O S Re-Double

All the re-doubles we have met so far have shown strength. There is a situation, however, in which a re-double is used, conventionally, as a *distress signal*. This would be a typical example:

You open 1 C on: ♠ K 10 3 ♡ A Q 6 ◇ K J 9 ♣ Q 10 4 2.

Your Left Hand Opponent doubles, partner passes and so does your Right Hand Opponent.

It is clear from the informatory double that the high cards are over you, and from the second defender's pass that the clubs are stacked. You can escape into 1 NT, but it would be better to play in a suit in which partner has four, perhaps even five cards. At least the trumps may break more kindly for him.

A re-double in this situation is an urgent call for help.

No confusion is possible between the S O S and the normal strength-showing re-double of a One bid. The latter is used when the bidding is still in progress. The distress signal is hoisted when a pass would close the auction.

Moreover, and this consideration is decisive, if you thought that you could make seven tricks by yourself in your suit, you surely would not think of re-doubling. Instead of giving opponents another chance, you would pass gratefully.

S O S After Butt-In

The same type of situation would arise if you intervened with 1 H over 1 C and a double by your Left Hand Opponent was left in. With

♠ A K 6 ♡ J 8 7 4 2 ◇ K 9 6 3 ♣ 7

you would send an S O S signal to partner, expecting him to call 1 S or 2 D, but prepared, if he insists, to play the hand in 1 NT. Even that might be preferable to 1 H doubled, since it is clear that the trumps are massed in one hand.

FREE BIDS

The modern tendency in expert bridge is to extend the use of the S O S re-double to one or two other situations in which obvious inferences should preclude the risk of a misunderstanding.

Confusion, however, can be dangerous, and above all, very expensive. Even players of experience will be wise *never* to use the re-double as a distress signal except in the clear-cut situations described above. With uncertain partners at rubber bridge, it is best to forget that the S O S signal exists—unless, of course, partner sends out the call for help.

12

PROTECTION

As the auction develops, a good bidder watches the ebb and flow of changing values. At times he holds back on a fair hand, suspecting that partner has next to nothing. At others, he comes in on a sketchy holding, inferring from the bidding that he will find partner with hidden treasures.

An obvious situation arises when Responder passes his partner's opening bid. The pass denies more than about 5 points. Opener can hardly have more than 20 and has probably a good deal less. It is, therefore, apparent that defenders can count on half the pack's strength between them—sometimes a little less perhaps, but most of the time, quite a bit more.

In consequence, if the fourth player has 10 points or so, he can usually rely on his partner to have the same—or better.

In such a situation it is proper to reopen the bidding on values which would not justify an overcall. Americans call this Balancing. The term in Britain is Protection—because the last player to speak protects his partner's pass.

Minimum for Protection

When an opening of, say, 1 H is followed by two passes, the fourth player at the table may bid 1 S on a good 8 or 9 points —something like: ♠ K 10 7 6 3 ♡ 8 2 ◇ A J 6 ♣ 10 8 3. With more he can usually double. With much more he doubles first, then finds another bid over partner's response. Or else, if he has a good, long suit, he makes a jump bid in the first place—*2 S*, after 1 D has been passed round to him, as in (3) page 113.

Protective Doubles

Any bid in fourth position, after two passes, is, on the face of it, protective, and a double is not *necessarily* stronger than any other bid. At the same time, the cheaper the bid the less strength it needs, and over 1 D the cheapest bid is 1 H, and over 1 H it is 1 S—not double.

Though, by itself, a double promises nothing special, it suggests greater strength, because it may be the first step in describing a good hand. A suit bid at the One level, by a player in a protective position, can hardly show a strong hand.

Protection at the Two Level

A protective position arises also, though less pointedly, when a simple raise is about to be passed out. This time, Responder promises something, so partner may not have very much, and as the level is higher, it needs greater strength to protect. Even so, with the right shape, 11–12 points suffice. This may be shaded further, on a 4–4–4–1 pattern, the singleton being, of course, in opponent's suit. After the sequence:

S	W	N	E
1 H	No Bid	2 H	No Bid
No Bid			

West may double on ♠ K 10 7 6 ♡ 7 ◇ K J 8 2 ♣ K J 7 5 and with: ♠ A 3 ♡ 7 6 4 2 ◇ K Q J 6 4 2 ♣ 2 he may come in confidently with 3 D. Not only is partner marked with some general strength on the bidding, but he is also likely to have one Heart or none—since opponents have shown eight or nine between them.

When Not To Protect

A bad time to reopen the bidding is when you hold the enemy's suit in strength and have little outside. Then it is best to be satisfied with a small bonus above the line. A double, as in (6) page 114 would be protective, not business. Partner would bid and instead of collecting points, you would be making a present to opponents.

Responses to Protective Bids

Like an informatory double, a protective double should have shape. But whereas an informatory double presupposes little in partner's hand, a protective double allows for certain values indicated by the bidding.

Therefore, when partner responds, he must show restraint. With 10 points or so he is only living up to expectations—justifying the protective double. It follows that he must not jump, as he would do over an informatory double, with less than, say, 12–13 and a respectable suit.

Factors which Condition Protection

The minimum for reopening the auction must always be governed by partner's standards for intervening bids. The requirements outlined above presuppose a reasonably conservative attitude. With a partner, who butts in lightly, it is not enough to have 9 points and the qualifications should be raised according to his habits.

Other factors, too, must be taken into account. Was the opening 1 C? Then fourth player will need more to reopen the auction. Partner could have come in so easily over 1 C. If he did not, there can hardly be much to protect. Over an opening 1 S the position would not be quite the same.

For similar reasons, vulnerability is an important consideration. Partner needs less for an overcall at favourable vulnerability than when the positions are reversed. His pass, therefore, is in less need of protection.

The modern tendency is to whittle down to the barest minimum the requirements for overcalls when opponents alone are vulnerable. With a partner who conforms to this trend, there is no obligation to protect on even 10–11, unless you have a good shape for a double or a respectable suit of your own.

Protection at Rubber Bridge

At rubber bridge, with indifferent partners, occasions for purely protective bids occur rarely. And if you fear that there

PROTECTION

may be some confusion between a protective and an informatory double, never protect at all, for you will lose more on the swings than you can possibly gain on the roundabouts.

For your own guidance, if you are ever in doubt, apply this test: does the double follow a bid made by an opponent? Then it is an informatory or a business double. A *protective* double —or any other protective bid—comes only *after two passes* and at no other time.

Protective Situations

At Love All, West deals and opens 1 D. North and East pass. South holds:

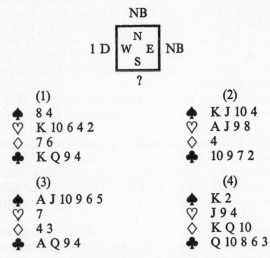

NB	
N	
1 D	W E	NB
S	
?	

(1)	(2)
♠ 8 4	♠ K J 10 4
♡ K 10 6 4 2	♡ A J 9 8
◇ 7 6	◇ 4
♣ K Q 9 4	♣ 10 9 7 2

(3)	(4)
♠ A J 10 9 6 5	♠ K 2
♡ 7	♡ J 9 4
◇ 4 3	◇ K Q 10
♣ A Q 9 4	♣ Q 10 8 6 3

(1) *1 H.* A minimum, but just enough for the cheapest bid.

(2) *Double.* The ideal shape. Note that the hand is improved appreciably by the middle cards.

(3) *2 S.* This shows that you have a good long suit and that you would have bid in any case—without being in a protective position.

(4) *1 NT.* Similar to an opening weak NT, shaded in view of the protective position.

113

PROTECTION

West raises East's opening 1 H to 2 H and this comes round to South, who holds:

(5)	(6)	(7)
♠ J 10 6 4	♠ A	♠ Q J 9 8 6
♡ 7 2	♡ Q J 10 8 6	♡ 6 5 3 2
◇ K Q 9	◇ K 4 2	◇ 7
♣ K Q J 4	♣ J 7 4 2	♣ A Q 3

(5) *Double.* Not much to spare, but you can stand, within reason, any response partner will make. If he has four Spades you may even have enough for game. Whenever in doubt about whether or not to protect, be guided by your holding in Spades.

(6) *No Bid.* Should you double, it will be protective, *not business,* and partner will find a bid—in Spades, no doubt.

(7) *2 S.* Partner can hardly have more than one Heart, since opponents have shown eight or nine. His hand promises, therefore, to be a good fit.

Responses to Protection

East, dealer, bids 1 H. After two passes, North doubles and East says No Bid. South holds:

(a)	(b)	(c)
♠ A 10 7 3	♠ A Q 7 5	♠ 7 3
♡ J 4 2	♡ 4 2	♡ A Q 10
◇ K J 9	◇ K J	◇ K Q 4 2
♣ Q 6 3	♣ Q J 7 6 2	♣ K 10 7 5

(a) *1 S.* If Partner is simply protecting on 9–12 points, a part score is the only prospect in sight. Should he find a second bid, it will be different.

(b) *2 S.* This justifies a jump, even after a protective double, and as always it is more constructive to show a major than a minor.

(c) *3 NT.* This was a maximum pass, of course, dictated by the weakness in Spades. The alternative to 3 NT is 2 H in the hope of reaching a slam in one of the minors, but at this stage the possibility is a little remote.

13

LEAD-DIRECTING DOUBLES

As we have seen in the preceding pages, a double can perform a variety of functions. In addition to the common penalty double, which raises the stakes as it were, we have met: the informatory double: the two-way double of a pre-emptive bid in a minor; the tentative double of a butt-in by Responder, and its counterpart, the co-operative double* by Opener of a rescue by the second defender; and also, in the last chapter, we met the protective double, after two passes, by the fourth player.

There is yet another type, quite distinct from the others—the Lead-Directing Double. The best known member of this family is the Lightner—so named after Theodore Lightner, a member of Culbertson's world-conquering team in the 'thirties.

The Lightner Slam Double

The Lightner operates only against slam contracts and its function is to call for an *unusual lead*.

A trump is barred, and so is the lead of any suit bid by either defender. If the auction is uncontested the Lightner double precludes the lead of an unbid suit, for that would not be in any way unusual.

In practice, the Lightner double is nearly always a demand for the lead of a suit bid by dummy.

It may be that East, who sits under South—declarer in most of the diagrams—can win the first trick by ruffing, if West can be persuaded to lead the suit. Or else he may have a King poised over a suspected Ace or an Ace-Queen over where the King should be.

* 'Co-operative Double' is used here in its natural sense. The term is applied sometimes to certain situations, which are far from clear cut and which arise too rarely to call for discussion in these pages.

LEAD-DIRECTING DOUBLES

Although there is, occasionally, confusion on the subject, the double does not call specifically for the lead of the first or second suit bid by the other side. Partner is generally in a position to work out what is wanted of him.

Making the Unusual Lead

This would be a typical example of a Lightner double:
Opponents bid as follows:

N	S
1 D	2 S
3 S	4 D
4 H	6 S

East doubles. Sitting West, you hold:

♠ 6 3
♡ Q 3 2
◇ 10 7 4 3
♣ Q J 10 9

Your natural lead is a Club. Clearly, however, East's double proclaims a void in Diamonds, so you proceed to give him a ruff with the opening lead. The effect of the Lightner double is to prevent the natural lead and to induce another.

Calling for the Unusual Lead

Now turn to the receiving end. You sit East with:

♠ K 9 7 6 5   ♡ 10 4 2   ◇ A 6   ♣ 7 6 2

Opponents bid:

N	S
1 S	3 D
4 D	4 NT (Blackwood)
5 H (Blackwood)	6 NT

You have a certain entry with the Ace of Diamonds and you

116

want the Spade King to be set up quickly, before that Ace goes. To make certain that partner opens a Spade you double.

The Ace of Spades may be over you, it is true, but North has shown two Aces, apart from opening 1 S, and it is a risk well worth taking.

Price of Doubling Slams

Of course, the defender, who uses the Lightner convention, must not double a slam unless he is prepared for an unusual lead. But that is no great price to pay for what can be, on occasion, a devastating weapon. A slam bid voluntarily, not as a sacrifice, rarely goes more than one down. And for an extra 100 points—50 non-vulnerable—the charge for doubling is utterly exorbitant. If opponents make the contract, they get a bonus (in a major) of 230, which, if they redouble, becomes 590. It is less prohibitive if opponents bid the slam in a minor, but bad enough.

Doubling Cue Bids

Doubles of high level cue bids, and that includes responses to Blackwood, should be lead-directing and nothing else.

If opponents are feeling their way to a slam in Hearts and one of them bids 5 D—or responds 5 D to 4 NT—it is worse than fatuous to double on: ♠ 4 3 ♡ 7 2 ◇ Q 10 9 6 5 4 ♣ K Q J. The hand will not be played in Diamonds, though if there were the least prospect that it might be, to put opponents off by doubling would be utter folly. Holding the hand given above, a defender wants his partner to lead a Club. Therefore, he should only double a cue bid—or a Blackwood response—in Clubs.

Doubling Low-Level Artificial Bids

The double of conventional game demand bids and responses has a different end in view. This time, the double is, in fact, based on length and the purpose is not so much to indicate a lead as to suggest a possible sacrifice to partner. If he has a distributional hand, with support for your minor, he may be able to take advantage of a good fit, and it costs nothing to tell him about it.

To a lesser extent, this also applies to doubles of the Stayman 2 C bid or to the 2 D response, especially when opponents use the weak No Trump. Here, however, the double usually suggests that the lead of the suit in defence may be desirable.

Lead-Directing Doubles of Game Contracts

A penalty double of a freely bid game contract, as distinct from a sacrifice, presupposes that the cards are well placed for the defenders—that their Kings are over the Aces and their A Qs over the Kings. Further, it is legitimate to assume that if a contract is doubled, the suits bid by declarer's side may break badly.

From all that it is a far cry to demand, as some players do, that in the event of a double, partner should *always* lead the suit bid by dummy. Such is not the case. If either defender has bid a suit, a double calls for the lead of that suit. If East doubles when no suit has been bid by the defenders, West should judge each hand on its merits. With a suit as good as: Q J 10 8 2 and a likely entry, he should lead his own suit.

I take two illustrative examples from *Card Play Technique*. (1) The bidding sequence is:

South	North
—	1 D
1 S	3 D
3 NT	No Bid

East doubles. It is impossible to construct a likely hand for West on which he should open a Diamond.

But

South	North
—	1 D
1 H	1 S
2 NT	3 NT

LEAD-DIRECTING DOUBLES

East doubles, and West has to find a lead from:

♠ 10 9   ♡ J 7 5 4   ◇ 10 8 4 2   ♣ Q 6 4

This time, the ten of Spades looks like a good lead—and West has no temptation to try any other.

In short, when defenders have not intervened, a penalty double may point to the lead of the suit bid by dummy. But it is only a suggestion and never a command.

14

SACRIFICE BIDDING

For all the hands that belong to the other side we must be prepared to pay something. It is often cheaper to concede a penalty than to allow opponents to make a part score, a game or a slam, and the essence of sacrifice bidding is to pay the right price at the right time.

It is generally accepted that it pays to go two down doubled, at equal vulnerability, to save a game and four down to save a slam—even five down, in fact, will show a small paper profit.

These figures, which are indisputable theoretically, should be treated with reserve at the Bridge table. All too often practice does not conform to theory.

To pay 500 for a vulnerable game saves only 100 or so. But every phantom sacrifice—when opponents would have failed in their contract—costs 600, for then we pay them 500 to save them from paying us 100. At aggregate scoring, even when the odds are 6 to 1 that the other side will make game, the sacrifice has little to commend it.

Other factors, it is true, are involved. By overbidding we may induce opponents to overbid, too, and that prospect alters at once the basis of the calculation. Broadly speaking, however, the emphasis should be less on how much we should pay for their game as on how likely they are to make it.

An accurate assessment depends on close co-operation with partner and underlines, once again, the error of butting-in without defensive values.

The Forcing Pass

In many competitive situations partner must be entrusted

with the ultimate decision and this often calls for a well-judged pass.

A pass can be absolutely forcing.

Two examples will suffice to show how—and why.

1. Partner opens 1 NT, which you raise to 3 NT. Your Left Hand Opponent bids 4 S and partner passes.

What are the inferences?

Since your side has contracted to make nine tricks at No Trumps, you can certainly expect to defeat 4 S. Why, then, does not partner double? The answer is that the penalty may not be big enough. He does not know. It depends, maybe, on whether your raise was based on all-round strength or on a long minor. You know more about partner's hand than he knows about yours, and in consequence, he refers the decision to you.

This pass is absolutely forcing. You can double or bid 4 NT, but whatever your holding, you cannot allow opponents to stay in 4 S undoubled.

2. Here is another situation:

Your side bids Spades. The other side bids Hearts. Over 4 H on his right, partner calls 4 S, and over 5 H on your right you call 5 S. Your Left Hand Opponent calls 6 H and partner *passes*.

Why?

There are three possibilities: (a) the hand belongs to you and they are sacrificing; (b) the hand belongs to them and you are sacrificing; (c) the distribution is so freakish that, for all you know, either side may be able to make twelve tricks.

Interpret partner's pass in the light of these three alternatives. (a) If opponents are sacrificing partner can obviously double. If he does not, it can only be because he sees prospects of a slam and wants you to decide. By inference his pass is stronger than a double since it invites you to consider bidding a slam.

(b) If the hand belongs to them and you were willing to sacrifice in 5 S against 5 H, it must be more profitable still to stop 6 H by calling 6 S. Why, then, does partner pass? Clearly, he sees some hope of defeating 6 H and is referring the matter to you. Unless you expect to beat the slam, you must sacrifice unhesitatingly. Once again, partner's pass is *unconditionally* forcing and you must not shirk your responsibility.

(c) If the hands are so freakish that either side may make twelve tricks with its suit as trumps, there can be no question of allowing opponents to buy the contract. The swing could be enormous and it is worth paying a big premium to ensure against it. Partner's forcing pass shows that he is in doubt. If you, too, are in doubt, you must bid 6 S. You have no choice.

Ensuring Against Swings

The modern trend, induced by the increasing popularity of duplicate, is to sacrifice readily. At rubber bridge a conservative policy pays better. But whatever the conditions or the method of scoring, there is a sound guiding principle: when in doubt, sit back on balanced hands and buy the contract when the distribution is freakish.

To miss a sacrifice, even a cheap one, can never be catastrophic. To find yourself at the wrong end of a swing—when they make game in one suit and you could have made one in another—can lose a match at duplicate and a lot of money at rubber bridge.

15

DECEPTION

'Technique without bridge psychology is of little value.' These words, written by Ely Culbertson nearly thirty years ago, have even greater force now. The general standard has risen steeply and mere competence no longer suffices for victory. To ensure success today it is necessary to induce errors in opponents, as well as to avoid them oneself.

Psychology has many facets, each one richly deserving to be studied separately. This cannot be attempted within the confines of a single chapter, but one aspect of the subject, Deception, is so closely woven into the fabric of the game that without it no textbook on bridge can be complete.

Tactical Deception

An example of deception, with which most players are familiar, occurs at rubber bridge, when one side is 60 up. Let us say that the part score is yours and that you are playing a weak NT. After partner has passed you can open 1 NT on as much as 20 points. Anxious to save the game or rubber, opponents may step in unwarily, laying themselves open to a heavy penalty. If they bid, you shed the sheep's clothing and double. The nature of your 1 NT is revealed, but only after the trap has been sprung.

Deceiving in Safety

Every deceptive manœuvre carries the danger of boomeranging on the deceiver. Partner, as well as opponents, is misled, and he may be the one to take action, carrying the bidding too high or raising the wrong suit or doubling at the wrong time: To deceive in safety, occasions must be picked when partner can do no harm. The camouflaged No Trump at 60 up is a good example, because partner can be deceived free of charge and with complete impunity.

The same example brings to light another basic feature of deception. Benefits accrue not only when it is perpetrated, but at other times, too, when no deception is intended.

Remembering the trap 1 NT, opponents may be over-cautious next time, when, perhaps, they have a cheap save. In fact, a few deals later, while an opponent is still smarting from the sting of a big penalty, you may snatch game or rubber by opening a sub-minimum No Trump. For deception works both ways and you can be weaker than you sound, as well as stronger.

Inhibitory Bids

Among the safest weapons in the armoury of deception are spurious trial bids and cue bids.

You open 1 D and partner raises to 3 D. Holding:

♠ 6 2   ♡ —   ◇ A J 10 7 6 4   ♣ A Q J 7 3

you may decide that you want to be in a slam and that you do not want a Spade lead.

Instead of bidding 6 D you first call 3 S. You cannot tell what partner will do and you are not really interested for your only concern is to inhibit a Spade lead. It will not come off every time, of course, but it is worth trying. You cannot lose—with an intelligent partner.

As before, the two basic conditions for successful deception are present. Partner, though duly deceived, can do no harm. And the benefits will not be confined to this deal. Opponents will wonder in future whether you are genuine or not and they may, in consequence, present you with unexpectedly favour-able openings. If a player impresses you as being unduly sus-picious, you may even coax a welcome lead out of him by making a cue bid on an A Q or K J x holding.

It should be emphasized that repetition inevitably reduces or nullifies the effects of deception. To ensure success the bait should be changed from time to time and the tactics varied, so as to keep the other side guessing—and therefore misguessing.

DECEPTION

Sowing Confusion

The next example, which I take from *Bridge Psychology*, introduces a new element: Confusion.

As South you hold: ♠ 7 6 4 2 ♡ Q 10 9 7 6 3 ◇ A K 6 ♣— and at favourable vulnerability you stretch a little to open 1 H.

The bidding proceeds:

South	West	North	East
1 H	1 S	2 H	3 S
?			

Two things are apparent.

(1) Opponents have the balance of high cards and good distribution, too, since one of them must be short in Hearts.

(2) Your partner is marked with one Spade or none and you can make a lot of tricks if you are allowed to buy the contract.

Can you persuade the other side to sell it?

One method is to pass and to wait for West's inevitable 4 S before coming in with Hearts at the Five level. This sequence may create the impression that you have no hope of game and are only sacrificing. The chances of being doubled may be better than if you call an honest 4 H first, then 5 H over 4 S.

An alternative stratagem is to call 4 C over 3 S. In theory this is a trial bid since the Heart suit has been agreed. In practice it is just an attempt to obscure the issue—to introduce confusion for its own sake.

Both opponents are marked with Clubs. Each, in turn, may fear that his side suit will break badly or that the Club honours will be misplaced, and if so, defence may appear to offer better prospects than attack. The spurious 4 C bid can help and it can hardly hurt.

And once again, the knowledge that you make such bids may lead opponents into error on occasions when you are genuine. To engender distrust in opponents is almost as important as to inspire confidence in partner. And the attempt to achieve both aims simultaneously makes the game richer and more interesting for both sides, and sometimes more profitable for yours.

16

BRIDGE AT THE SUMMIT

In the hands which follow, all played by Terence Reese and Boris Schapiro in the World Championship of 1965, the reader will meet in a new context many of the points examined in the foregoing pages.

Two of the hands brought by the accusers in their indictment of Reese and Schapiro before the World Bridge Federation bear directly on the Principle of Preparedness discussed at the outset of this book.

This was deal 25 in the Britain-Italy match.

```
                    ♠ Q 8 4
                    ♡ J 10 4
                    ◇ K Q 5 2
                    ♣ J 6 5
  ♠ A K J 10 2          N           ♠ 9 7 6
  ♡ Q 9 7 2         W       E       ♡ A 8 6 5
  ◇ 7 6                 S           ◇ A J 9
  ♣ 4 3                             ♣ A 9 7
                    ♠ 5 3
                    ♡ K 3
                    ◇ 10 8 4 3
                    ♣ K Q 10 8 2
```

EW Game.

Garozzo	Reese	Forquet	Schapiro
South	*West*	*North*	*East*
		No	1 C
No	1 S	No	1 NT
No	2 NT	No	3 H
No	4H		

On the Acol system, played by Reese and Schapiro, East's

hand is a king or so under the required strength for a vulnerable No Trump. An opening of One Heart might pose an awkward rebid problem. Hence the Prepared Club on a 3-card suit. Had Schapiro passed his partner's 2 No Trumps, not an eyebrow would have been raised. Sensing, perhaps, and rightly as it proved, that the aggressive Italians in the other room might bid game, Schapiro made one more effort—3 Hearts. It is this bid which gave rise to the accusation of signalling. The ACBL (American Contract Bridge League) booklet on the World Championship calls it "a most unusual manoeuvre." It does not explain why. If, in fact, Schapiro's hand is worth any sort of bid over 2 No Trumps, 3 Hearts would appear to be much the best. It allows a 4–4 Heart fit to come to light without precluding a final contract of 3 No Trumps, 3 Spades or 4 Spades.

The Italians also reached 4 H, but with West as declarer. On the way round, East made a cue-bid of 4 C, which Harrison-Gray doubled for a lead (see page 117). Ignoring the double, Harrison-Gray's partner, Kenneth Konstam, opened the King of Diamonds, allowing D'Alelio to make his contract. Against a Club lead, Schapiro had no chance.

The reader will note that in the bidding both sides stretched their values by a point or so. The reason lies in the method of scoring in World Championships. International Match Points —known as IMPs—put a premium on vulnerable games, which are worth bidding even when the odds are tilted against declarer.

A different facet of Preparedness comes under the spotlight in deal 36 of Britain's match against the United States.

BRIDGE AT THE SUMMIT

```
                    ♠  1 0 7 2
                    ♡  K 8 4
                    ◇  A 8 6 4
                    ♣  9 8 5
♠  4                      N                  ♠  K Q J 9
♡  J 6 5 3 2        W          E             ♡  A 10 9 7
◇  Q 5                    S                  ◇  J 10 9 7 3
♣  K Q J 10 4                                ♣  ——
                    ♠  A 8 6 5 3
                    ♡  Q
                    ◇  K 2
                    ♣  A 7 6 3 2
```

Mrs. Hayden	Reese	Becker	Schapiro
South	*West*	*North*	*East*
	No	No	1 S
No	1 NT	No	2 H
No	4 H		

In the closed room, Schenken, America's East, also opened
One Spade in preference to the natural bid of One Diamond,
which might have proved awkward had partner responded
Two Clubs. Leventritt bid Two Hearts and the Americans
sailed gaily into Four Hearts.

How was it, asked the accusers, that in the other room,
Schapiro found a rebid of Two Hearts over Reese's One No
Trump? Why didn't he call Two Diamonds? Did he know,
through an improper signal, that his partner had five hearts?

The answer for the defence was that had Schapiro known of
five hearts opposite, he would have hardly elected to open
One Spade. He would have either called One Diamond, allowing Reese to show Hearts at the one level—or he might have
called One Heart. That, on mature reflection, was perhaps the
best opening in any circumstances.

Moreover, had Reese known that Schapiro had four Hearts,
he would have doubtless responded Two Hearts—as Leventritt,
the American West did in the other room—instead of calling
an unorthodox One No Trump.

BRIDGE AT THE SUMMIT

A variant on the theme of Preparedness occurred on deal 22 of Britain's match against Italy.

```
                    ♠ Q J 9 3
                    ♡ A 10 9 4
                    ◇ —
                    ♣ K 10 5 4 3
♠ K 2                    N              ♠ 8 7 6 5 4
♡ K Q J 6           W       E          ♡ 8 5
◇ K 9 8 6 4             S               ◇ A Q 5
♣ Q 2                                   ♣ J 8 7
                    ♠ A 10
                    ♡ 7 3 2
                    ◇ J 10 7 3 2
                    ♣ A 9 4
```

Garozzo	Reese	Forquet	Schapiro
South	*West*	*North*	*East*
			No
No	1 D	No	2 D

The accusers argued that Reese, according to his own lights, made an unprepared bid. His correct opening, they said, was not One Diamond but One Heart.

Reese replied that since his partner had already passed, he was under no obligation to prepare a rebid (see page 12). Had Schapiro called Two Clubs, the most awkward response, Reese would have passed. Why, then, should he bid his shorter suit first?

Opening the higher-ranking of two touching suits, when it is shorter than the other, is a matter of style. There is a case for it if the minimum requirements for biddable suits are strictly observed. Then it helps to bring to light a 4–4 fit should responder feel hesitant in showing a diaphanous major.

The manoeuvre has less to commend it with a partner who is determined to show his major, regardless of quality, whenever he can do so at the One level. After partner has passed, the principle of Preparedness should never be pushed too far.

The danger in opening 1 Heart is not that the partner will have a doubleton, for then he can do little harm, but that with three Hearts he may give jump preference, on the next round, over 2 Diamonds and that this may prove embarrassing.

The question of biddable suits comes to the fore on the next example, deal 23 against Italy.

♠ Q 8 7 5	N	♠ K 3 2
♡ 9 4 3 2	W E	♡ K J
◇ Q J	S	◇ A 10 7 6
♣ Q 8 6		♣ K 10 7 5

Garozzo	**Reese**	**Forquet**	**Schapiro**
South	*West*	*North*	*East*
No	No	No	1 D
No	1 S		2 S

Should not Reese have responded One Heart instead of One Spade, giving himself an extra chance of finding a major suit fit (see page 15)? Or did he know that his partner had only two hearts? Reese replied that he disliked bidding bad suits on bad hands. In competitive situations it could be highly dangerous.

Again, this is largely a question of style. A study of Reese's methods shows that he often leans to the side of conservatism.

Many of the hands submitted to the Court of Enquiry in London had no special meaning in themselves. They were introduced solely to establish—or to refute—a particular pattern of bidding in regard to the Heart suit.

On deal 42 of the Anglo-American match both Easts, Boris Schapiro for Britain and Howard Schenken for America, opened One No Trump. The East-West hands were:

♠ J 5 4	N	♠ K 7
♡ 9 8 6 3 2	W E	♡ J 5 4
◇ 5 4	S	◇ A Q 10 8 9
♣ J 9 8		♣ A Q 7

The American West passed. The British, Terence Reese, called Two Hearts. Did he know that his partner had three Hearts? Or would he have made the same bid opposite a doubleton?

Before passing judgment, the reader may find it helpful to look up "Weakness Take Out" on Page 31.

Among the deals cited by the accusers was 117 against Italy.

The East-West hands, which alone matter ,were:

♠ K 9	N	♠ A 10 7
♡ A J 10 9 5	W E	♡ 8 7 4
◇ K 8 7	S	◇ 10 5 3
♣ A J 5		♣ 10 4 3 2

Forquet	Schapiro	Garozzo	Reese
North (dealer)	*East*	*South*	*West*
No	No	No	1 H
1 S	No	No	2 H
No	No	2 S	

How did Reese come to rebid Two Hearts? Should not he have doubled or bid One No Trump or even passed? Or did he sense that Schapiro had three hearts? That was the suggestion when the hand was submitted to the Court of Enquiry. Reese pointed to the solid texture of his suit.

The Defence could counter also with Board 76 against the United States.

♠ K Q 7	N	♠ 9 8 4
♡ A J 8 5 2	W E	♡ 6 4
◇ Q 9 3	S	◇ J 7 6 3
♣ 8 2		♣ Q 5 4 3

Reese opened the West hand with One No Trump. Becker, America's North, doubled and after two passes, Reese rescued himself into Two Hearts. This was doubled by Dorothy Hayden America's South, and cost Britain 900—five down. Had Reese known of the worthless doubleton opposite, would he have bid Two Hearts?

Both sides at the BBL Enquiry put forward deal 137 in the match between Britain and Italy. This was the question: what should Schapiro, sitting East, open on:

♠ A K 9 5   ♡ A 9 6 5 4 2   ◇ 9   ♣ A K

and which way would his decision be influenced by the knowledge that partner had a void in hearts?

The definition of an Intermediate Two Bid on the Acol system, followed by Reese-Schapiro is: "Eight playing tricks and a good suit, usually a 6-card suit. Or else it is a two-suited hand. Apart from playing tricks there must be controls and high cards in at least two suits . . . . . ." (see page 68).

It is possible to argue either way. Opposite a void, the Heart suit obviously fails to live up to expectations and ceases to be a "good suit." But then, if partner has no Hearts, he may well have a wretched hand with four or five small spades, and if so, East wants him to keep the bidding open for one round—which he must do after an Acol Two bid.

Schapiro opened One Heart. Reese passed and the British scored 110. In the other room, the Italians bid Four Spades and made 12 tricks.

West (Reese) held:

♠ 10 4 3 2   ♡ —   ◇ Q 6 5 2   ♣ Q 9 8 7 5

The result is purely incidental, but what bearing, if any, has this hand on the "cheating" controversy?

Boris Schapiro's bidding on deal 35 against Italy has been the subject of criticism. These were the Reese-Schapiro hands:

Reese			Schapiro
♠ J 6 3		N	♠ A K 8 4 2
♡ K J 9 6	W	E	♡ A
◇ A 8 3			◇ Q J 10 4
♣ J 7 5		S	♣ A Q 9

After two passes, Schapiro opened One Spade and raised Reese's response of One No Trump to Three No Trumps.

Why did Schapiro bid Three No Trumps instead of Three Diamonds? He needed so little opposite for a slam. Five Diamonds to the King and the Queen of Spades might have sufficed, yet Three No Trumps could go down on a heart lead. Or did Schapiro know that Reese had four Hearts? That was the suggestion.

Reese answers (Bridge Magazine, September, 1965):

"The argument is nonsensical for if East knows that West holds four hearts he can bid Three Diamonds, knowing that partner will take appropriate action."

The Italians reached Six Spades and went one down.

BRIDGE AT THE SUMMIT

Deal 39 against the United States illustrates the essential conservatism of Terence Reese, something which should be borne in mind when judging the Buenos Aires hands as a whole.

```
                    ♠ J 4
                    ♡ J 7 5 2
                    ◇ A 9 6 4 3
                    ♣ 9 7
♠ A 10 9 2              N              ♠ K 6 3
♡ K Q 4 3        W         E          ♡ A 10 9 6
◇ J 8 7 2              S              ◇ 10
♣ 4                                   ♠ A 10 8 6 2
                    ♠ Q 8 7 5
                    ♡ 8
                    ◇ K Q 5
                    ♣ K Q J 5 3
```

Hayden	Reese	Becker	Schapiro
South	*West*	*North*	*East*
1 C	No	1 D	No
1 S	No	1 NT	No
2 D	No	No	2 H
No	No!	No	

Schapiro's bid of Two Hearts is an example of Protection—or Balancing—described in Chapter 12. Opponents have disclosed strictly limited values and he is entitled to expect some help from partner. Even so, Reese has surely enough to raise him. Compare his extreme caution with the boldness of the Americans. This was the bidding sequence in the other room:

Harrison-Gray	Laventritt	Rose	Schenken
South	*West*	*North*	*East*
1 C	Double	1 D	2 D
3 D	No	No	4 D
No	4 H		

Unlike Reese, Leventritt comes in with a double of One Club and now nothing can stop Schenken. He cue-bids opponents's suit twice, Two Diamonds, then Four Diamonds, forcing his partner to game.

BRIDGE AT THE SUMMIT

In both rooms, ten tricks were made with Hearts as trumps, but only the Americans, of course, scored game.

If Reese and Schapiro had guilty foreknowledge of each other's cards, and more especially of their respective holdings in Hearts, their bidding on this hand makes no sense at all.

The defence put forward deal 126 v. Italy.

```
                    ♠ Q 8 5 4
                    ♡ A Q 10
                    ◇ 9 5
                    ♣ J 7 5 4
    ♠ K 6 3            N            ♠ J 7 2
    ♡ K 4         W       E         ♡ 8
    ◇ Q 10 6 3         S            ◇ A K 8 7 4 2
    ♣ K Q 8 2                       ♣ A 10 6
                    ♠ A 10 9
                    ♡ J 9 7 6 5 3 2
                    ◇ J              Love All
                    ♣ 9 3
```

Schapiro, East, opened One No Trump, as dealer, and Reese put him up to Three No Trumps. South opened a low heart and proceeded to collect the first seven tricks.

The opening One No Trump was hardly an inspired bid by any standard. But that is not the point. The case for the Defence is that if Reese and Schapiro signalled to each other their length in Hearts, they would not have landed in Three No Trumps—certainly not played by East. It was not even a case of bluffing for they held the balance of the cards..

In the other room, the Italians made, Four Diamonds, scoring 130 on the East–West cards.

One of the targets of the accusers was deal 50 in Britain's match against the United States.

```
                    ♠ A 10 7
                    ♡ J 8 5 3
                    ◇ Q J
                    ♣ K J 5 3
♠ 7 3              N              ♠ Q J 9 8 6 4
♡ A Q 9 7 4    W       E          ♡ —
◇ A 8 6 5         S              ◇ 10 9 7 4 3 2
♣ 9 4                            ♣ 10
                    ♠ K 5
                    ♡ K 10 6 2
                    ◇ K
                    ♣ A Q 8 7 6 2
```

Reese	**Hayden**	**Schapiro**	**Becker**
South	*West*	*North*	*East*
			3 S
Double	No	4 H	No
No	Double		

Where did Schapiro, sitting North, find his Four Heart Bid? That was the objection raised by the accusers.

In the other room, Rose, Becker's opposite number, also opened Three Spades. Unlike Reese, however, Erdos, the American South, passed and it was left to North, Petterson, to contest the auction by doubling. Erdos now bid Four Hearts and Harrison-Gray, West, doubled for Britain. The result was the same in both rooms—Four Hearts doubled, one down.

Both pairs, Reese-Schapiro and Erdos-Petterson, used the same defensive weapon against pre-emptive openings—the optional double.

Both sides took risks, but then the justification for pre-emptive bids is that they compel opponents to take chances, whether they enter the bidding or allow themselves to be shut out.

Petterson, North, took a greater risk then Reese, South, for he had the poorer hand. Schapiro had something to spare for his bid opposite a double. It should be noted, too, that the British pair followed the Italian variant of the optional double. This promises support for *two* suits. Schapiro knew, therefore, that unless Reese had good hearts he would be strong in the minors and, that of course, would have suited him admirably.

In the rough and tumble of everyday bridge, superior bidding and dummy play are usually decisive. At the summit, where all the contestants are accomplished technicians, the issue often hinges on psychology and tactics. Certain of the bids, which have been in the forefront of the Reese-Schapiro controversy, fall under the category of psychics discussed in Chapter 15. On board 30, the second board which he played against the Americans in partnership with Schapiro, Reese introduced "a diversion", to use his own expression.

Reese		Schapiro
♠ 10 9 5 3	N	♠ Q J 7
♡ K J 10 8 6	W E	♡ Q 7 4 2
◇ 9 4	S	◇ 7 6 3
♣ 6 5		♣ K 10 4

Schapiro dealt and passed. Dorothy Hayden, South bid One Club and Reese overcalled with One No Trump, which Becker doubled. After two passes, Reese bid Two Diamonds.

What was the meaning of Reese's One No Trump? And what did Two Diamonds signify? Reese and Schapiro were playing the Gardener No Trump overcall, a two-way bid, which could be genuine or purely obstructive. What, asked the accusers, was Reese's escape suit? Hearts? If so, how did he know that Schapiro had four hearts? Or was he courting a 700 or 900 penalty?

Reese could have re-doubled for a rescue, of course, asking partner to call his longest major. His intentions will never be known for Becker did not double Two Diamonds. Defending his bid in Le Bridgeur (September 15th, 1965) Reese says: "I had noticed that Mrs. Hayden and Becker were often embarrassed by semi-psychics." Moreover, in the light of partner's pass a game for the other side was virtually certain and a slam by no means improbable. It was worth taking a risk.

BRIDGE AT THE SUMMIT

In the event the Americans reached Six Clubs and made it. In the other room, the British bid Six Diamonds making all thirteen tricks.

It was the turn of the Americans to attempt a piece of deception on deal 58.

```
              ♠ Q 8
              ♡ K 10 4
              ◇ K 4
              ♣ A K J 8 5 3
 ♠ 5 3 2           N           ♠ A K 10 7 4
 ♡ 7 3 2        W     E        ♡ 8 5
 ◇ 10 7 6 5 3      S           ◇ Q 8 2
 ♣ 4 2                         ♣ 10 9 5
              ♠ J 9 6
              ♡ A Q J 9 6
              ◇ A J 9
              ♣ Q 7
```

With East-West remaining silent, the bidding in the two rooms was:

Britain		U.S.	
Reese	**Schapiro**	**Erdos**	**Patterson**
South	*North*	*South*	*North*
1 H	3 C	1 NT	3 C
3 H	4 H	3 H	4 C
5 D	5 H	4 S	6 C

Schapiro's Five Hearts over Reese's cue bid of Five Diamonds denied the ace of spades. With a singleton, he would have bid Six Hearts, not five, while with Kx he would have tried Six Clubs or Six No Trumps to let the opening lead run up to his hand. Having pinpointed two losers in Spades, the British pair had no trouble in keeping out of a slam.

In the other room, Erdos made an inhibiting bid (see page 124) of Four Spades in the hope of preventing a Spade lead. Holding both the ace and king of the suit, Rose preferred to believe what he saw to what he heard and the Slam went down.

The accused came under fire on deal 127 in Britain's match

against Italy.

```
                    ♠ A K 9 7
                    ♡ Q 9 8 5
                    ◇ A 4
                    ♣ 9 6 3
  ♠ Q 5 4               N              ♠ J 10 8 3 2
  ♡ A J 7 3         W       E          ♡ 4
  ◇ K 7 5               S              ◇ J 6 3
  ♣ A K Q                              ♣ 10 8 5 2
                    ♠ 6
                    ♡ K 10 6 2
                    ◇ Q 10 9 8 2
                    ♣ J 7 4
```

Garozzo	Reese	Forquet	Schapiro
South	*West*	*North*	*East*
No	1 C	Double	1 H
2 D	2 NT	No	3 C
No	No	No	

In years gone by the bid of a major on a singleton or doubleton over an informatory double used to be a routine psychic intended to prevent opponents from getting together in their predestined trump suit. Such psychics carry little danger for no experienced partner is likely to be misled. Knowing that any bid over a double proclaims weakness and even dire distress (page 94), he will not believe everything he hears. This, of course, applies in equal measure to the other side, and since no one is likely to be deceived, this particular manoeuvre is rarely used these days in good company. Reese himself describes it as "a baby psyche."

The only interest in Schapiro's bid, harmless if fatuous in itself, is its significance in the light of the signalling charges. If he knew that his partner had four hearts, why should Schapiro seek to deter the Italians from running into an unlucky trump break?

Another point is made for the defence. If Reese knew that Schapiro had a singleton heart, why didn't he double 2 Diamonds? As the cards are, the penalty would have been 800.

BRIDGE AT THE SUMMIT

Is this, in fact, a hand for the accusers or for the accused?

One of the exhibits at the enquiry was deal 18 against Italy. Schapiro, East, dealt and opened One Spade on:

♠ A 9 8 7 2   ♡ 9 2   ◇ K Q 10 5   ♣ A 3

Garozzo, South, doubled. Reese passed and Forquet called Two Clubs. What should Schapiro do now? There is a good case for passing and no strong objection to Two Diamonds. Boris Schapiro bid Two Hearts. As on the last hand, the ostensible purpose of the psyche was to make it hard for the Italians to find a heart contract.

```
                        ♠ Q 10
                        ♡ K 10 7
                        ◇ 9 8 7 4
                        ♣ K J 7 4
        ♠ J 6 5                         ♠ A 9 8 7 2
        ♡ 6 5           N               ♡ 9 2
        ◇ J 3 2       W   E             ◇ K Q 10 5
        ♣ 10 9 8 6 5    S               ♣ A 3
                        ♠ K 4 3
                        ♡ A Q J 8 4 3
                        ◇ A 6           Game All.
                        ♣ Q 2           Dealer: East
```

Garozzo	Reese	Forquet	Schapiro
South	*West*	*North*	*East*
			1 S
Double	No	2 C	2 H
2 NT			

The accusers contend that because he knew the heart position, Schapiro had both the incentive to psyche in hearts and the assurance that he could do so in safety since there was no danger that Reese would raise him on a doubleton.

The defence counters with the argument that if cheating is assumed, Reese, not Schapiro, was the man to psyche in Hearts on the way round, especially as he could stand 2 Spades comfortably, if doubled.

There is, perhaps, a more compelling argument for the defence, though it was not brought out at the enquiry. For

Schapiro's psyche to succeed, he had to find partner with at least three hearts. Otherwise the Italians would have nine between them and no one could seriously hope to talk them out of that. In the event, of course, that is precisely what happened. For once, the wily Italians were caught in the toils of their system and stopped inexplicably in 2 No Trumps. But could Schapiro have foreseen it? Is it not more likely that he introduced a "diversion", to obscure the issue—to introduce confusion for its own sake (see the last page of Chapter 15).

17

FLASHBACK AND POSTSCRIPT

The last chapter was written before the 'Not Guilty' verdict of the Tribunal set up to enquire into the allegations of cheating against Terence Reese and Boris Schapiro. Almost every board on which hearts were mentioned was brought up at the enquiry. I have presented to the reader in Chapter 16 the hands which were most hotly debated at the hearings in London and which received most prominence in the American Press.

The charge, made during the closing stages of the 1965 World Championship in Buenos Aires, was that the British pair held their cards in such a manner as to indicate their respective holdings in the heart suit. An American magazine described this as "finger exercises". Two fingers showing over the backs of the cards was the alleged signal for a doubleton. Three fingers were supposed to denote three hearts and four fingers, four hearts.

That was the accusation made by two American players and by the English-born Bridge Editor of the *New York Times*. At a hastily summoned meeting in Buenos Aires, the World Bridge Federation accepted it. A subsequent enquiry instituted by the British Bridge League and conducted by Sir John Foster, Q.C., M.P., assisted by General Lord Bourne, over a period of 14 months, exonerated the accused.

The British Bridge League accepted immediately (on 9th August, 1966) the findings of the enquiry. A year earlier, before the enquiry had started in earnest, the American Contract Bridge League accepted the views of the World Bridge Federation.

From the first, the Buenos Aires Affair has been bedevilled

by a series of inexplicable contradictions.

Among those who claim to have seen the signals, the alleged "finger exercises", are bridge personalities of the highest repute on both sides of the Atlantic. Yet no one, on either side, has been able to explain why one of the world's most experienced and sophisticated partnerships should practise so crude and clumsy a method of cheating. Many of the world's leading players have been suspected in the past of signalling. None of them have been suspected of signalling so badly. Why, then, should two of the best players be the two most inept cheats of all time? It made no sense.

Inside this enigma was wrapped a riddle. Assuming the desire to cheat, why pick on the heart suit? Would it not be more profitable to exchange illicit information about voids, singletons, doubletons or hand patterns in general? Ingenious theories have been put forward in support of the hearts-mystique, but not one was entirely convincing. Again, it made no sense.

It may be that some of the contradictions in the Buenos Aires Affair will never be resolved. All humans err some of the time and some humans err most of the time, and already memories are becoming blurred. But the cards themselves do not and cannot err and no deal will be blurred by time. Every one is on record, as fresh today as when the hands were taken out of their slots in May, 1965.

Having examined the hands, the reader will be in a position to form his own views. He need not hesitate to judge the examples of "summit bridge", described in Chapter 16, in the light of the basic principles of bidding explained in the previous 15 chapters; for tension may run high at a World Championship and tactics are dictated by circumstances, but the basic structure of bidding remains the same at all levels.